In Case
I Should Forget

by
Brian Russell

Grosvenor House
Publishing Limited

The right of Brian Russell to be identified as the author of this
work has been asserted in accordance with Section 78
of the Copyright, Designs and Patents Act 1988

The book cover is copyright to Brian Russell

This book is published by
Grosvenor House Publishing Ltd
Link House
140 The Broadway, Tolworth, Surrey, KT6 7HT.
www.grosvenorhousepublishing.co.uk

A CIP record for this book
is available from the British Library

ISBN 978-1-83975-060-1

ACKNOWLEDGEMENTS

When I first started to write this story it began as nothing more than the intention of recording a few recollections of my life that I hoped might one day give my children, Christian and Natalie, a better insight into what their father did for a living.

The initial notes that I scribbled were nothing more than a few random memories but as they grew I decided to place them into some semblance of chronological order and to this purpose I turned to Barry Wilkinson who helped me fill in a number of gaps that I had forgotten during my Dark Ages and Influence days. Other things then began to spring to mind. Silly things, like the time in 1966 when the band were considering changing our name from the Dark Ages and a daytime work colleague suggested we call ourselves the Red Mollie Whatnots. Thank you Robert Common but I think that Influence had more of an edge to it.

From there I sought help from Pete Holmes, Nick MacCartney and Mick Elliott and the Edentree era took shape. It was during this time that I found myself being able to recall more and more detail and, with the exception of some further assistance from a few others for the later years, everything else you read is my own rambling.

During the best part of the five years that it took me to complete I had rewritten my memoir several times. Each time I tried to improve on my previous efforts until finally it was finished. From my original self-typed memories I decided that, having come this far, it might be a good idea to try and have my story released in book form. After receiving encouragement from two other national publishing companies I decided to place myself in the hands of Grosvenor House Publishing,

There are four other people who deserve a special mention for their valued contribution to this work.

Originally this book was to be called The Story of a Nobody. Someone I met on holiday a few years ago suggested that In Case I Should Forget might be a better title.

I offer my utmost gratitude to Chris Rackham, who painstakingly proofread my final efforts of what you are about to read.

David Clayton has been a constant encouragement to me throughout this entire venture and I thank him for his kind words in the Foreword of the book.

Finally the actual book cover had to be designed and I am delighted that I was able to leave this in the charge of my son Christian, a computer graphic artist.

I hope that I have done them all justice.

FOREWORD

Brian and I have been musing for years that we should write down everything before we start forgetting it. Read on, because he's only gone and done it!

The fact that he and I spent around a decade working together is only a small part of his story but for both of us they were heady days and not a conversation goes by without one of us trawling up some hysterical anecdote the other has forgotten.

Together, we lived and breathed Norwich Artistes, the entertainment agency we had "inherited" and having spent all day fixing up entertainment hither and thither, would spend most evenings running the nightly cabaret show at Talk of East Anglia. He was the compere, I was the DJ It was hard work and long hours, but in hindsight it was fun, so much fun. If we'd realised how special it was at the time, we'd have written it down there and then. Thankfully Brian has done the next best thing in this book.

But Brian's history is far broader than that, rubbing shoulders with the pop and rock stars of the sixties, flirting with national TV stardom and landing a record deal with his band, Edentree. Chart-topping success was but a contract away, or so it seemed. It wasn't all plain sailing. There was often disappointment but there was always a laugh along the way.

In Case I Should Forget captures several eras of the entertainment business from the fabled working men's clubs of the north east, through TV talent shows and on to the launch of Norwich's own fondly-remembered cabaret club on Oak Street.

I departed the agency business in 1983 and realised my ambition of a broadcasting career. Brian carried on building a deserved reputation as the area's most experienced entertainment agent and consultant.

Whether it's all about luck, happenstance, talent or sheer staying power, you can make up your own mind, but Brian is still there at the helm of Norwich Artistes applying some five decades of knowledge and experience to the business we call "Show."

David Clayton

IN CASE I SHOULD FORGET

It has been said that there is a story in each and every one of us. If that is the case then my mother would certainly have had a story to tell.

She was born Rose Ann Hill in 1922. She came from Blackburn in Lancashire and left her hometown at the age of fourteen along with four of her siblings. Her mother, Amelia, gathered up the five of her six children and fled her husband. Their destination was Norwich, where Amelia took up with the man she had come to Norfolk to be with.

My mother was placed into a school in the district of Hellesdon, less than a mile from where I now live, where she proved to be more academically advanced than some of the other children of her age. Consequently, she spent, what was to be the last two months of her education, teaching her classmates French before finally leaving school and taking up full time employment at a local chocolate factory.

She married young and soon after, her husband, an air pilot, was reported missing during a flying mission over Burma. His body was never found. She later met my father and they married in 1946 spending the next sixty-five, and somewhat largely argumentative years, together. Dementia, in my mother's case, vascular, eventually took them both over and they had to be taken into care. By coincidence they both passed away on exactly the same day, 20th May – my father in 2013 and my mother four years later.

The thought that any one of us could end up with dementia has spurred me into writing this book. People have often said to me that I have led an interesting life so here goes.

These are my memories – this is my story.

1

I was delivered into this world on the 26th February 1947 at number 8 Home Street in Norwich. I was the first born to my parents, Rose and Walter, and was christened Brian Russell Tubby, Russell my middle name in memory of my father's brother. From Home Street we moved into a two bedroom council flat in Hall Road where my brother Peter was born in 1950 and from there to a three bedroom semi-detached house in Tuckswood Lane which saw the arrival of Anne and Sylvia my two sisters. The house became my parent's home for the next fifty eight years up until the time they were no longer capable of looking after themselves. After I had become involved with the music business in the mid-sixties I changed my name by Deed Poll to Brian Russell.

We were never what you might consider a close-knit family. I was closer to my mother than my father. She loved music and used to sing along to the latest songs on the wireless. I listened and at an early age I knew many of the songs off by heart. From her I gathered tales of *The Ugly Duckling*, *The Owl and the Pussycat* and *The Little Old Lady who swallowed a Fly*. One of my mother's particular favourites was a monologue by Stanley Holloway about a young lad named Albert and a lion called Wallace. Years later, as she was approaching the end of her life in the care home, *Albert and the Lion* always managed to break through the barrier of her dementia. It never failed to bring a smile to her face whenever I recited it to her.

My father was a gambler and he indulged in his favourite pastime with people who included "Ramo," "Al Fonso," "Tex the Yank" and "Laughing Peter," names that conjured up all sorts of wondrous images to a highly impressionable lad like me, not yet in his teens. Sometimes my father didn't come home from work on a Friday night and my mother knew that a card school was taking place somewhere. One Saturday morning she sent me into a snooker hall, still bearing all the scars of wartime bombing, to look for my dad whilst she and my brother Peter waited outside. There was the smell of stale tobacco in the air and the tall intimidating shadows of people hovering above me as I searched for my father amongst the snooker tables in the darkened hall.

The gambling occasionally took place at our house where a great deal of money often changed hands and winning or losing could dictate my father's mood. Certainly a heavy loss could easily ignite the fuse of his short temper and he was known to resort to heavy handed measures, the signs of which I quickly learnt to read and give him a wide berth.

* * *

From an early age I spent weekends with my father's parents. On Friday afternoons, when school had finished, I would board the bus to their prefab on Heigham Street. The bus stopped directly outside and my grandfather could usually be found busying himself in his garden. He had lost an eye and his hip dysplasia rendered him unfit for work. My grandmother worked and when she came home the weekend began.

My grandparents had a television set, something of a luxury in those days, and this only added to the magic of those weekends and the long school holidays. I would sit glued to the black and white screen watching the *Michael Holiday Show* after Don Lang and his Frantic Five had entertained on *the 6-5 Special*. The adventures of *Lassie,* the collie dog, sometimes made me sad and I laughed at the antics of Lucille Ball in *I Love Lucy* and George and Gracie in *the Burns and Allen Show*.

2

It was at the prefab in Heigham Street that my imagination began to wander. I was happy in my own company and spent hours immersed in story-writing. I wrote about Lord and Lady Pendragon and a murder that took place at Pendragon Hall, their ancestral home. The story was written in play form and included production notes within the narrative, such as enter stage left or exit stage right. My grandparents listened with interest as I read them the latest episode of my unfolding drama.

That prefab became my haven. Its small back garden doubled as a football pitch for a kick-about and a rickety wooden shed, leaning against a neighbouring wall, housed a cage in which lived my ever-growing population of pet mice. Inside the prefab and taking pride of place on the wall above the fireplace, was a framed tapestry simply proclaiming the hand-stitched word *Mother*. A maple leaf was embroidered in one corner of the fabric symbolising the country of its origin. My father had brought it back from Canada where he had spent months in a sanatorium recovering from tuberculosis during his time in the RAF.

M *is for the million things she gave me*
O *means only that she's growing old*
T *is for the tears she shed to save me*
H *is for her heart of purist gold*
E *is for her eyes with love light shining*
R *means right and right she'll always be*
Put them all together they spell mother – a word that means the world to me.

Whilst in the sanatorium, my father had met and fallen in love with a nurse with whom he wanted to remain in Canada. This account of my life may not have been written at all had it not been for the fact that my grandmother had tragically lost her youngest son Russell through illness and did not intend on losing another. She insisted that my father return home to England when his time in the RAF was up.

There were unexpected surprises waiting to be discovered inside the prefab. Once, while rummaging through the contents of a side-board in the hallway I came across a small box and, upon opening it, I found myself gazing at my grandfather's glass eye.

My greatest find of all was an ancient wind-up gramophone. Inside the wooden cabinet were the tiny needles that fitted into the open horn trumpet together with a collection of long forgotten records that were gathering dust in their sleeves. They included *The Mountains of Mourne,* an Irish folk song and a Victorian tearjerker from Arthur Blackwell called *Ring down the Curtain I Can't Sing Tonight*. The gramophone had been idle for years but I became fascinated as I wound the handle and listened to those crackly voices and sounds from a bygone age.

* * *

In the fifties a new kind of music called Rock and Roll exploded onto the scene. Saturday mornings were soon taken up by shopping with my grandmother who would treat me to the latest 45 r.p.m. (revolutions per minute) vinyl record release. Those 45's were smaller and more robust than the old and brittle 78's that I had been playing. My record collection soon grew and eventually Frankie Lane, Donald Peers and the Andrew Sisters became relegated to the bottom of the pile as Elvis Presley, Bill Haley and Tommy Steele took centre stage. When I started singing along to the latest hits, my grandmother decided that I should have a guitar to accompany me. I never did learn to play it but it gave her immense pleasure as I strummed away tunelessly whilst singing and mimicking my pop idols.

'You spoil that boy,' my grandfather would say.

2

My eleventh year arrived and with it came the final term at primary school. It was also time for me to sit the dreaded Eleven Plus – an examination that I showed very little interest in and as a result I spent the remaining four years of my school life at Lakenham Secondary Modern.

I soon made friends and a gang of us used to congregate outside my house at the bottom of the lane. We played football on the green in the middle of the estate and games that began with five or six of us would end up with larger numbers as more turned up and joined in. The games continued throughout the day until darkness finally caused the matches to be abandoned.

Girls had been of little interest but all that changed by the time I reached thirteen. There then came the one-night stands, and even more serious relationships that could last for weeks. To those girls that I encountered along the way, through those awkward fumbling days and nights of discovery and courtship, I would like to offer a big thank you for being there at my awakening.

At sixteen years of age I had left school and considered myself to be an adult. Some of my friends were still in their final year at school when I started work in the accounts office of an upmarket footwear store in the centre of Norwich. The four pounds a week I earned was immense compared to the pocket money my friends received and it would be my treat for fish and chips all round on a Friday night when payday came.

* * *

Football became a big part of our lives. In 1963 I was part of a team that played in a five-a-side league at the local Lads Club. A Sunday newspaper, *The People*, sponsored a national knock-out competition with the finals played, and televised, at Wembley. We entered the competition and won all our regional matches and, in doing so we qualified for London where we were beaten by a very good side from Welling in Kent.

I also played grown-up eleven-a-side football for my local Sunday team – a team which over the years produced some very good players.

Mike Plunkett was an inspired goalkeeper and Kevin Dale an accomplished centre-half whilst the Dowson brothers, Rodney and Terry, controlled the defence and midfield respectively. Inside-forward Clive Radley went on to play cricket for both Middlesex and England and big John Tythcott, our centre-forward, plundered goals unmercifully. Two members of our team however were outstanding.

Tony Woolmer was a young art student when he made his league debut for Norwich City away to Wolverhampton Wanderers. Norwich were beaten 4-1 but Tony scored their only goal that Saturday afternoon before turning out for Tuckswood Hotspur the following morning.

The other was Peter Batch, as gifted a footballer as you were likely to find. Peter had scored many of the goals for our five-a-side team during our cup run before a chronic attack of asthma prevented him from playing in the final at Wembley. He was later approached by the Scunthorpe United manager Ron Ashman who wanted to sign him to form an attacking partnership alongside an up and coming player called Kevin Keegan. No amount of praise is enough for Peter who might have gone on to forge a career for himself in the professional game had it not been for his asthma.

* * *

By 1964 music had taken a firm grip on my life. My record collection had grown considerably and I was also now the proud owner of a blue and grey, plastic coated, Dansette record player. John Wilkes was a friend of mine and we both had similar tastes in music. The two of us would get together at his house and record ourselves singing Everly Brothers songs on John's Grundig tape recorder.

One day John told me that he had joined a local pop group as their singer and invited me along to one of their practice sessions. By now John and I had progressed beyond the Everly Brothers and we likened ourselves more to Simon and Garfunkel.

During the group practice that night we sang *The Sound of Silence*. It must have made a suitable impression on drummer Barry Wilkinson, lead guitarist Derek Pickering, bass player Nick Day and rhythm guitarist Alan Holmes because they asked me to also join the band. I instantly agreed and John and I decided that we needed to invest in some sound equipment.

We paid a visit to a local music shop and picked out two Reslo ribbon microphones, which were identical to the ones that we had seen the Beatles use. We also decided to buy a fifty-watt Treble and Bass Selmer Public Address system. John's half share of our financial commitment needed the consent of his mother but she refused to sign the hire purchase agreement resulting in him quitting the group soon after and leaving me as the sole lead singer.

Another person I met at that first practice night was Nick Moore. Nick was the elected manager of the group due to his contacts in the business – he worked with a girl called Helen, whose boyfriend Barry had become the drummer. Barry was the proud owner of a new drum kit and both Derek and Nick already had smart-looking guitars and amplifiers. I now owned a microphone and a PA system. Alan Holmes' equipment was homemade but it made do and we now considered ourselves to be a proper group. All we needed to make it complete was a name.

We thought long and hard and eventually came up with the Dark Ages.

* * *

I had been working for about eighteen months when my boss asked me to enrol for an accountancy course at the local college. Although his request was undoubtedly made with the thought that promotion within the office would eventually follow I had given little consideration as to what my long term future might hold. As far as I was concerned life was for living and I was getting on with it.

After another wage increase at work, together with a sideline I had in buying and selling clocks and watches, my fortunes began to prosper. I could now afford to buy handmade suits and I had my first car, a white Ford Popular. The only downside was that I had not yet passed my driving test.

There were two other members of our clan who also owned cars and the three of us often talked of venturing further afield from the local places which we used to visit on a regular basis.

And so it was that one August, along with Michael "Barney" Barnes, Peter Batch, and David "Smithy" Smith, I took off for a fortnight's holiday to Blackpool. With qualified driver "Barney" sitting in the front beside me we travelled to the Lancashire resort in my Ford Popular – L Plates on display and heavily ladened down with tent and camping equipment.

Another time we paid a visit to Torquay when Nick Moore, "Smithy," "Barney" and yours truly travelled in the spacious comfort of Nick's Wolseley 6/90, an ex-police car. We stayed in Torquay for less than an hour before realising that the Devonshire coast offered very little in the way of attraction so, deciding on somewhere that we knew would be more appealing, we then proceeded to drive the three hundred miles north to Blackpool instead.

During one trip to the Isle of Wight, two members of our party ran out of money before the holiday had come to an end.

They decided to go home early leaving Terry Dowson and me on the island without transport. By the time Saturday, the final day of our stay, came around our own funds were almost exhausted and we were left with no alternative but to hitch-hike back to Norwich.

Lifts were few and far between as drivers repeatedly ignored our thumbed requests and we eventually arrived home in darkness having spent the best part of a day on the road. It was not until later that we found out our plight had not been helped by the fact that, in the early hours of our Saturday morning departure, two convicts had absconded from Parkhurst Prison on the Isle of Wight. Police had advised the public that the escaped prisoners would probably try and make their way to the mainland and not to approach them as they were considered to be dangerous.

* * *

Back in Norfolk, when Saturday nights came around, sometimes as many as six of us would manage to squeeze ourselves into "Barney's" Ford Anglia and visit the surrounding village dance halls that were always heaving with girls. There was occasionally some friendly rivalry between us, the "City Slickers" and the local male community, the "Country Yokels." On occasions however the rivalry wasn't quite so friendly if we were deemed to steal the attention of their women folk. We would then be forced to make a timely exit.

On one such occasion we managed to escape to the relative safety of the Ford Anglia. After Barney had started the engine and plunged the car into gear, we realised that we were not moving. Our pursuers had grabbed the back bumper and lifted the vehicle off the ground. Barney revved the engine a second time and the exhaust backfired engulfing those behind in smoke and fumes. They released their grip and the wheels hit the ground. There was a strong smell of burning rubber and we screeched away back to the safety of Norwich.

That night I couldn't help but notice the group who had been playing. They hadn't been threatened as outsiders and had been accepted by almost everyone in the local community whereas we had not. Simply, through the music they played, they had gained, not only adoration from the girls, but also appreciation and respect from the men.

I envied the way that they had been looked up to and the status they seemed to have achieved just by being on that stage. I imagined that one day that would be us; we too would be regarded as something that people could look up to. We would be the Dark Ages – that is when manager Nick comes up with a booking.

3

It was a midweek band practice and by now we had about twenty numbers rehearsed to a creditable standard. Our songs consisted basically of Rock and Roll with a little bit of Soul music thrown in. Suddenly the door opened and Nick came bursting in.

'We've got a booking!' he gasped.

We were to appear at a school dance as the support band to Barry Lee and the Planets. They were a local outfit from Aylsham and regarded as one of the leading groups in East Anglia. There was much to be done before our debut. We had a name and a repertoire but what to wear? We eventually decided on black polo neck sweaters and black trousers and the Dark Ages were ready for the road.

The night of our first live performance came and went in a blur. There had been the initial excitement of seeing our name on a poster beneath Barry Lee and the Planets and then our actual entrance onto the stage. I tapped the microphone and muttered the obligatory 'Testing one two' into it before we launched into *Johnny B Goode*. We finished thirty minutes later with *A Land of a Thousand Dances* and at the end of the night we collected our fee of three pounds. Our general feeling was that it had been a successful first booking despite making a few mistakes. There was one incident however that could easily have brought our performance to a standstill and could not be overlooked.

It happened midway through a number when Alan Holmes had broken a guitar string, which he was prone to doing on a regular basis. The breaking of the string was unfortunate enough but brandishing the offending piece of wire in the air and bringing it to the attention of the entire band, as if we hadn't noticed, was unforgivable and so we decided that the Dark Ages would in future continue without the services of a rhythm guitarist – sorry Alan.

We were fortunate that our bass player Nick had a father who was an outstanding musician. Lew Day was a guitarist who had moved to Norwich from London some years earlier and he played in the house band at the Samson and Hercules, a local Mecca ballroom. Lew always managed to find the time to be on hand if needed and he offered help and advice whenever we rehearsed new material.

We had become adventurous with our music. The repertoire was now more expansive and diverse as we added numbers by bands such as the Animals and Manfred Mann together with upbeat dance floor fillers by black artistes who recorded on the Stax label. Drummer Barry was also a big fan of some groups from the West Coast of America and subsequently songs from the likes of Love and the Doors also found their way on to our playlist.

Together, as the Dark Ages, we had been going for almost a year in which time we had appeared at local dance halls, schools and community centres. We felt the time had come for a change of name and searched for something simple that rolled off the tongue and had more of an impact. We eventually agreed on Influence.

* * *

1966 was upon us and the country was gripped with World Cup football fever. Early one midweek evening I was sitting alone at the bar in Backs, a popular city pub. Suddenly a voice behind me asked if I could tell him where the Melody Rooms were. I turned around to discover a short stocky man who introduced himself as Phil Beevis. He told me that he was in the music business and managed a group from his local town of Long Melford in Suffolk. He was in Norwich to try and get them a booking at the Melody Rooms. I told him that I was also in a group and as Phil had no transport I offered to drive him to the club.

That night, at the Melody Rooms, Phil must have made a suitable impression because, not only did he get the booking for his group, soon after he moved to Norwich and became the booker of bands for the venue. He proved himself to be well connected within the music industry and brought names such as the Who, Cream, Traffic, Jethro Tull, Rod Stewart and Fleetwood Mac to Norfolk.

Phil also had an eye for spotting up and coming groups. One such group was booked at the Melody Rooms on a date that happened to coincide with the club owner Geoffrey Fisher's birthday. Geoff said that he wanted a more recognisable name for the occasion and the legendary sixties singer PJ Proby was added to the bill. Proby arrived in Norwich late afternoon on the day and, after his sound-check, he decided to hang around for a drink or two. Two drinks became a few more as he enjoyed a conducted tour of some of the pubs in the city.

PJ Proby was a great singer who had previously recorded demos for Elvis Presley in his native America before finding record success for himself in Great Britain. He was also a charismatic entertainer and that night he delivered an outstanding performance.

And since you may be wondering, the other group, who had become reduced to a supporting role that evening, was Procol Harum. They were little known when Phil had originally made the booking but were riding high at number one in the music charts with *A Whiter Shade of Pale* at the time of their Melody Rooms appearance.

Phil Beevis and I became good friends as he began finding work for some of the local groups. For Feel for Soul, a seven-piece band, he secured a thirty day British tour as the backing group for the Drifters.

Rick Sheppard, Bill Fredericks, Charlie Thomas and Johnny Moore, who made up the Drifters, flew into London from America early one morning and were taken to Streatham Locarno where they were appearing that same evening. There they were introduced to their backing band for the very first time. The Drifters had with them a tape machine containing all their hit records and Feel for Soul learnt the entire repertoire during the day before embarking on the nationwide tour that night.

Bumbly Hum was another band that Phil had taken under his wing. The line-up included Dave and John, two imports from New Zealand, and the people of Norwich took to the group who developed a fondness for knickers! Young enthusiastic ladies would be de-briefed prior to the performance and the fruits of the bands plunder would then be stapled to the sides of the stage. The girls would queue for this pleasure and then queue again outside the dressing room afterwards to claim their garments back.

* * *

Our band Influence was going from strength to strength. We were increasingly in demand throughout the Home Counties but the travelling sometimes proved difficult for me, being the only member of the band who had to work on Saturdays. Longer journeys to venues such as the Hermitage Ballroom in Hitchin, the Embassy Suite in Colchester and RAF High Wycombe in Buckinghamshire meant earlier departures from Norwich and there were occasions when I crept out of the office mid-afternoon, hoping that my absence would not be noticed during the remainder of the working day.

We considered that we were definitely on the way up when we appeared alongside the Nashville Teens (*Tobacco Road*), Little Jimmy Dickens from the US (*May the Bird Of Paradise Fly up Your Nose*) and Clodagh Rodgers (*Come Back and Shake Me* and *Jack in the Box*) – all of whom were popular recording names of their day. Bookings were coming in on a regular basis as more people got to know about us – people like "Smithie," who drummer Barry had met in his local pub, and whose claim to fame was that he had once supposedly managed Crispian St Peters of *The Pied Piper* and *You Were on My Mind* fame.

Our local status continued to grow after we had appeared at the Orford Cellar, Norwich's answer to Liverpool's Cavern. We were also booked alongside the Bee Gees at the Floral Hall in Gorleston. They had just scored a hit with their first UK single *New York Mining Disaster 1941*.

We turned up at the Floral Hall mid-afternoon to find the venue closed and the Bee Gees arrived soon after. They happened to have a ball in their van and, with nothing more to do than kill time until we could get in the building to set up, we enjoyed a game of football in the car park.

Robin, Barry and Maurice Gibb had yet to morph themselves into the iconic band that they would eventually become during their phenomenally successful *Saturday Night Fever* days and, together with Australian drummer Colin Peterson as an official member, they were then a four-piece band. I remember how tight their vocal harmonies were and at the end of the night Barry Gibb strummed a few chords on his guitar.

'It's an idea I have for a song' he said. That song would eventually become *World*.

* * *

Phil Beevis was coming up with more and more challenging bookings for us. We played new venues in Chelmsford, Clacton and the surrounding Essex area together with USAF bases and prestigious London nightspots, including the celebrated Blaises in the heart of Kensington. Phil also sent us, accompanied by six go-go dancers, for an audition at the 100 Club in London's Oxford Street when he heard of a potential tour of American air bases in the Far East.

Not long after this, bass player Nick Day decided to join his father in the Mecca dance band and we were fortunate in finding a more than adequate replacement in Mick Brighton. Our entourage on the road had increased in numbers and we now had two roadies. Nigel and Roy would come along to our gigs, carry some equipment, drink some beer and chance their arm with the local female talent.

We continued to find ourselves on the bill with some well-known acts. We supported Geno Washington and the Ram Jam Band, the Flower Pot Men – fresh from their *Let's Go to San Francisco* chart success, and Georgie Fame and the Blue Flames. There was however one unexpected and very nervy occasion that we experienced during an appearance in Dereham with Cat Stevens.

The problems began when his backing band didn't appear to be over familiar with his songs. After twice playing the wrong introduction into one of his biggest hits *Matthew and Son*, Cat Stevens was singing so badly out of tune that he eventually abandoned the number and ended his performance prematurely. This resulted in pandemonium amongst the audience who included some leather clad bikers. They followed in hot pursuit as Cat Stevens, together with his band and us, somehow caught up in the frenzy, fled downstairs and locked ourselves in the dressing room until the bouncers arrived to restore order.

We never did understand how a very mod-revered Cat Stevens had managed to attract such a gathering of rockers amongst the audience that night. I think in the end we came to the conclusion that it was probably down to a general lack of other things for people to do in that sleepy Norfolk metropolis.

4

Something new was happening to music and fashion through-out the country. Psychedelia, or Flower Power as it became known, had arrived and with it, a different sound from American West Coast groups was sweeping the nation. Grannies had their wardrobes raided by both sexes who came in search of long abandoned moth-eaten fur coats that had suddenly become the fashionable thing to wear. Kaftans, beads, bells and flowers were must-have accessories which completed the look. Barefoot hippies went about their business of preaching peace and free love and everywhere in the air was the smell of incense from Joss sticks.

With this new movement came drugs. Cannabis, in parti-cular, could be obtained with very little difficulty.

In complete contrast to the so-called "Beautiful People," there were also the more riotous types of bands. One outfit in particular was The Crazy World of Arthur Brown, who became noted for their highly outrageous stage performances.

It was alleged that in 1967, whilst being lowered by crane above the audience and onto the stage at Windsor Race Course, Arthur had urinated on the crowd. Whether this actually happened or not didn't seem to matter as stories such as this only helped to enhance the band's reputation which in turn resulted in them becoming an even bigger public attraction.

***

I have always considered that the job of a front man in a band is primarily to entertain. Knowing how to work an audience is just as important as the musicians who know how to create the sound behind him and the antics of the front man are very often the memory that the public take home with them. Noting all the changes that were taking place and our band having supported The Crazy World of Arthur Brown and seen their spectacle first hand, we certainly weren't going to allow this latest phenomenon to pass us by.

We therefore decided on a change of direction and we introduced something completely different into our act.

Apart from their style of dress, one very predominant feature of the Flower Power people was the way they painted themselves in vividly bright colours. I decided to follow suit and jam jars filled with water colours, together with paint brushes, were placed along the front of the stage at the venues where we appeared. For us to do justice to our intended show-piece we needed a song that reflected the current mood and trends of the day and we settled on a number called *Signed DC* by Love. This was not one of my favourite songs; I found it to be a dirge but the lyrics were in tune with the moment.

Sometimes I feel so lonely...
My comedown I'm scared to face...
I pierced my skin again Lord...
No-one cares for me

During this tale of misery, I removed my shirt and invited girls from the audience to come on stage and paint my face and body. We had achieved a visual and effective piece of stage performance that became an instant hit with the people and an integral part of what we did. It was particularly popular at one venue in Clacton where George the proprietor would greet our arrival:-

'You are doing the painting bit tonight aren't you?'

Derek Pickering's guitar solo in *Signed DC* screamed away as I stood in nothing but my white jeans. Enthusiastic females, let loose with a paint brush, would then daub me into a kaleidoscope of colour. George, armed with his own paint brush, would join the girls on stage where he would add his own creative contribution to the montage on my anatomy – and invariably he would end with a swish of his brush across my nether regions.

"The Paint Scene", as it became known, had certainly proven to be more popular than we ever imagined but it did sometimes have its setbacks. Not all of the venues where we played were equipped with washing facilities and I would sometimes arrive home later that night looking as if I had been involved in a road accident.

Despite the countless times we performed the number my feelings for *Signed DC* have never changed. It was later in life, after I had rediscovered the song on YouTube, that I listened to hear if it really was as bad as I remembered it to be all those years ago. The answer is a most definitive yes!

* * *

Feel for Soul were about to be given a boost with the arrival in Norwich of their new singer. Raymond "Boz" Burrell came from Holbeach in Lincolnshire and had previously sung with the Kings Lynn based group Tea Time 4, later to become known as the Boz People. The band had split following a disagreement between Boz and the keyboard player Ian McLagan regarding its musical direction. McLagan then left to join the Small Faces and it was rumoured at some point that Boz was to replace Roger Daltry in the Who.

Boz was welcomed by everyone. He was a bit of a nomad and sometimes slept on the kitchen floor of Phil's flat in Earlham Road and once or twice on the settee at my house. In general he stayed anywhere and with anyone who would have him. I enjoyed his company and sometimes drove him back home to visit his mother who lived in Saracens Head on the Norfolk and Lincolnshire border.

Boz became an instant hit with Feel for Soul and had the ability of getting a tune out of almost any instrument he picked up. He once bought a penny whistle from the local market and, that night on stage, he improvised a solo on it in the middle of *Harlem Shuffle*.

There was an occasion when Influence was due to play at USAF Lakenheath in Suffolk and Mick our bass player became unavailable. Boz offered to stand in.

'But you don't play bass,' I said.

'It will be okay,' replied Boz. 'Just get me a guitar.'

So we got him a guitar and he played. On reflection all this time after, the fact that nothing in particular springs to mind about that night suggests that everything must indeed have been okay, just as Boz had said it would be.

I would like to think that evening at Lakenheath saw the birth of a musician who, only a few years later, would grace the stages of arenas and stadiums throughout the world as the bass player with super groups King Crimson and Bad Company. It was some time later, in the eighties, when our drummer Barry went to Wembley with his son Carl to see Carl's favourite band Bad Company. I hope that Barry let it be known to Carl that Boz had cut his teeth for future stardom by once playing a gig with Influence!

* * *

I found myself becoming less and less enchanted with the conventional world. Boredom had crept in at work and I made the decision that the accountancy course was not for me. Music was playing such a big part of what was going on around me and I was so absorbed in my new life that everything else seemed to pale into insignificance. I was hanging out with people who did the things I wanted to do – wiling away the hours by immersing themselves in their music. As my association with them grew so came the temptation to smoke marijuana.

There was one person, after he had stayed at my house overnight, who next morning asked what had become of a small cube of silver tin foil that he had left on the bathroom window sill. My mother told him that she had tidied the room and, thinking it was rubbish, had thrown it out of the window. There followed a mad dash out into the back garden where Prince our dog was stretched out on the lawn. After a thorough going over of the area where it was considered the cube would have landed, the search was finally abandoned with the reluctant assumption that Prince must have eaten it.

* * *

Eddie Oates was an old friend of Phil Beevis and also came from Long Melford in Suffolk. From time to time Eddie would unexpectedly show up in Norwich and stay for a few days. He came from good stock – he was a descendant of Captain Lawrence "Titus" Oates, the man who had abandoned his tent during Scott's expedition to the South Pole in 1912, walking out to his death in order that his companions might have sufficient provisions to survive.

Eddie was an accomplished drinker and it was light-heartedly suggested that the fact he kept company with the actor Oliver Reed might have something to do with it. Eddie's party piece was to grip a pint glass full of beer between his teeth, tilt his head back and, without using his hands or spilling a drop, empty the glass in less than two seconds.

One afternoon we were gathered in a pub where Eddie performed his feat to an enthusiastic crowd of fellow drinkers. Phil Beevis got caught up in the revelry and decided that Eddie's talent deserved a larger audience. Phil made a telephone call to Anglia Television and a few hours later Eddie Oates appeared on TV, demonstrating his party piece for the umpteenth time that day, as the final credits for the regional news programme began to roll.

* * *

Boz and I took ourselves off to London to visit the Marquee Club in Soho's Wardour Street. Situated nearby was La Chasse, a small drinking club and a popular haunt for people in the music business. Jack Barrie was a businessman from Kings Lynn who had an entertainment agency called ABC Promotions. He had previously managed Boz before moving to London in 1967 to run La Chasse. Jack was a respected figure in the business and had also managed the Marquee for a while.

Established bands, together with new up and coming outfits, played the Marquee on a regular weekly basis and we planned our visit for the night when Long John Baldry and his band were appearing. John was regarded as the godfather of the Soho blues and soul music scene and he was also gay and highly outrageous. One of those outrageous moments occurred when we walked into the Marquee whilst John was on stage. He spotted Boz and immediately, and very graphically, openly propositioned him over the microphone.

Long John Baldry helped launch the music careers of two members of his band. Reg Dwight the piano player, who would later reinvent himself as Elton John, and vocalist Rod "The Mod" Stewart were two success stories waiting to happen. After the Marquee had closed for the evening we all piled into La Chasse where there was a fully loaded jukebox blasting away. It was there that I spotted a popular macho television name of the day in the company of rent boys.

* * *

Séances were a popular pastime in the sixties. People gathered round tables and experimented with an upturned glass, the letters of the alphabet, numbers 0 to 9 and the words Yes and No spread out before them. A few of us tried unsuccessfully on several occasions to make contact with "The Other Side."

One night we were travelling back from Great Yarmouth. Between the village of Acle and Norwich is the tiny community of North and South Burlingham. Here there are two churches; one in normal service and the other in ruin, the tower having collapsed in 1906. The congregation finally abandoned it in 1936 for the other church less than a mile along the road. In the ruin, Victorian tiling formed an aisle up the middle to the off centre chancel arch. The roof timbers were mostly still in place although completely unsafe. There were broken ledger stones and you could see into the vault beneath the chancel floor.

It was in the early hours of the morning when I parked the group van, after someone had suggested it a good idea to conduct a séance in the ruined church. We considered that in such surroundings with the appropriate atmosphere we might have more chance of getting through to the spirit world. Squatting on the floor, and with a shadowy view into the vault, we improvised an Ouija board and began our quest to contact the dead.

'Is anybody there?' a voice from our group asked and we were startled by the flapping wings of an owl we had disturbed, that clearly wanted to play no part in our proceedings.

'Is anybody there?' someone asked again. Suddenly Keith screamed that he had seen "The Angel of Death." He became hysterical and we began to panic. We fled the church and back to the sanctuary of the van where Keith had to be restrained as he lashed out with his arms and legs. Phil Beevis had a very anxious sound to his voice.

'Quick put the light on!' he exclaimed but when I clicked the switch the interior of the van remained in darkness. That did it – by now we were all convinced that we had received a visitation, and that someone, or something, was in the van with us. I drove at high speed back to Norwich where we spent the remainder of the night at Phil's flat.

The next morning we awoke to bright sunshine and blue skies. Keith had no recollection of what he might, or might not have seen, the previous night. I discovered the reason why the van's interior light had failed to work was because Keith's flaying legs had managed to kick the bulb out.

What more is there to say about the séance? Did we really make contact with "The Other Side?" Probably not and in the end we put it down to our imaginations, fuelled by the atmospheric setting, and possibly some other substances as well.

We certainly did some very silly and dangerous things in those days. There was a time when we found ourselves at the harbour of the seaside town of Gorleston. It was the middle of the night and Boz decided it a good idea to try and catch some fish. As we had neither a fishing rod nor a net this should have proven an impossible task but, with our imaginations running wild, improvisation was again the order of the day. With the aid of a fully extended microphone stand, and a screw driver taped to one end, I was held by my ankles from the edge of the pier whilst attempting to harpoon plaice that were floating on the surface of the water below.

Outside a Yarmouth amusement arcade I managed to get myself wedged inside a children's Doctor Who Dalek. Someone then deposited a coin in the slot and the apparatus swung into life. People passing by considered highly amusing watching me trapped inside the Dalek which was now spinning around booming 'Exterminate, Exterminate' from its speakers.

Not long after Boz left Norwich. His departure was almost as sudden as his arrival and there he was gone. Raymond Burrell's ongoing journey eventually led him to fame and, I would like to think, fortune. Our paths never crossed again and I was saddened to learn of the heart attack that caused his death at his Spanish home in September 2006.

5

Phil Beevis carried out his business from his upstairs flat on Earlham Road. There were times when his plans were highly optimistic, and had very little chance of succeeding, but Phil was forever the opportunist. He never gave up trying to achieve success for the people he believed in.

I was with him the afternoon he sat at his desk, Marlborough cigarette in one hand and telephone in the other, trying to persuade a Top of the Pops producer that his latest band was worthy of an appearance on the programme. The Precious Few had just released their version of *Young Girl* in the UK following Gary Puckett and the Union Gap's original recording that had topped the American charts.

* * *

Geoffrey Fisher's son John, along with his wife Veronica ("Ronnie") and sons Carl and Mark returned home to Norwich on New Year's Day 1967. They had returned from Singapore, where they had lived while John had been in the Royal Navy.

Geoffrey's business portfolio included Club America, two public houses, a coffee bar and the Melody Rooms. John Fisher became involved in the latter and it was there that he met Phil Beevis. Sometime after they got together and formed an entertainment agency. They named the business Norwich Artistes.

Up until then my life had predominantly been taken up with the band but there was now another influence in my life.

* * *

I was first introduced to Lyn by John Wilkes who knew one of her flatmates. At the beginning my friendship with her was purely that but it gradually developed into more of a steady relationship. The regular practice nights with Influence became less frequent and in late 1967 we all decided that we'd had enough and it was time to finish the band.

It had certainly been an experience that none of us could possibly have imagined when we first started out and it was satisfying to realise just how far we had managed to take the journey. Our playlist, which had begun as basic rock and roll and rhythm and blues, had developed into a repertoire of quality numbers. Sam Cooke's *Another Saturday Night*, Dusty Springfield's *Wishing and Hoping*, Dobie Grey's *The in Crowd*, *Rescue Me* by Fontella Bass, the Lovin' Spoonful's *You Didn't Have to Be So Nice*, *Going Back* by the Byrds and Neil Diamond's *Girl You'll Be a Woman Soon* were just some of the classics we performed that spring to mind. We had started out as four raw and naive individuals and had become a band that had experienced both the highs and lows – from the village halls in the outback of Norfolk and Suffolk to the upper crust of London's SW7.

Unlike our first ever booking, I am unable to recall our very last appearance together. I would like to think that it might have been in Clacton, and dear George's final assault on me with his paint brush.

It is an amusing thought but *Signed DC*? Oh dear!

Barry Wilkinson, Derek Pickering and I did stay together for a while longer when we briefly became part of a band called Amalgamation. The band had been formed by keyboard player Bren and girl singer Sam and also included Julian Revell and Chris Green, two of the brass players from Feel for Soul.

Amalgamation quickly built up a repertoire of numbers but we had performed only a handful of bookings together when I was asked to join the Alex Wilson Set, later to be renamed Kiss. They were a six-piece outfit consisting of some very highly rated musicians and I joined as their intended new singer after Derek Driver had announced that he was leaving. Derek then changed his mind which resulted in me playing second-fiddle, and very much a bit part in the line up. It was an unsatisfactory situation all round – the other band members had been together for quite some time and I was the complete outsider.

Just as I was contemplating whether or not to stay with them fate played a hand.

6

I was at the Melody Rooms one night when I happened to come across Tony Woods who was the manager of a group called the Caste. I had met the group on a previous occasion when Influence appeared alongside them at the Garibaldi Ballroom in Great Yarmouth.

The Caste had made local news by having a record released on the President label. The song was called *Don't Cast Aside* and it had received good reviews together with some national radio airplay. The band had publicly stated that they were optimistic about the record's success and hoped one day to be able to turn professional. Tony told me that Jim Duncan their lead singer was leaving and they were looking for someone to replace him. He asked what I was doing now that Influence had split up and I told him nothing much – which is what it felt like with the Alex Wilson Set. Tony suggested that I go along to one of the Caste's practice nights and have a run through with some of their numbers.

The following week I met up with the group in the back room of a local pub. Lead guitarist Nick MacCartney, bass player Mick Elliott, keyboard player Roger Cooke, drummer Pete Holmes and roadie John Wallis were an amiable lot and we hit it off from the very beginning. John Wallis had been affectionately nicknamed "Don't Know" due to the negative response he gave to practically every question put to him. As well as being the roadie he had also proven himself to be an accomplished song writer having co-penned, along with Nick MacCartney and Pete Holmes, *One Step Closer*, the B Side of *Don't Cast Aside*.

The Caste's collective vocal ability, together with the material they performed, was a lot different to what I had been used to with Influence. Then I had been the main singer with backup harmonies from Barry Wilkinson. The Caste produced a strong four part vocal harmony, Mick Elliott being the only non-singer, and they featured songs by the Beach Boys and the Four Seasons. I was familiar with many of the numbers they did and we gradually worked our way through the list. At the end of the evening they asked if I would be interested in joining them and I had no hesitation in saying yes.

They told me that, within their previous line-up, there had been something missing which, following Jim's Duncan's leaving, the band had set out to address. Jim was a good singer but he was not a front man and that was the reason why I had been brought in.

So there we were, a band with a national record release and bookings coming in at a steady rate. That was as high as our expectations could possibly reach, or so we thought.

But things were about to change.

* * *

Jack Barrie had formed his entertainment business in Kings Lynn, along with his partner Colin Atkinson, in 1964 and, raising their profile, they became known as ABC Promotions in 1966. They took on offices in Chappel Street and brought in Barry Tyler to run the agency side. The office represented a number of local groups including Barry Lee and the Planets. The band had turned professional and followed a similar direction as the Barron Knights and the Rockin' Berries by introducing comedy routines into their act. The combination of both music and comedy enabled them to find new work outlets on the national club and cabaret circuits. They changed their name to the Barry Lee Show and through Barry Tyler's skilful handling, together with introductions to some of London's biggest booking agents; they found themselves on theatre bills alongside household names such as Tom Jones, Engelbert Humperdinck, Dusty Springfield and the Walker Brothers.

Barry Tyler had expressed an interest in taking over the Caste and so we parted company with our manager Tony and joined the roster of ABC Management. We were told that our future might be better served by working towards the cabaret side of the business and so we decided to change our name and include some comedy in our act.

We became the Brian Russell Showcase. Pete Holmes and I were on a similar wavelength regarding humour and we both felt we were capable of coming up with suitable comedy material.

Barry Tyler liked the sound of the Brian Russell Showcase.

'That's a name that people won't forget in a hurry,' he told us. That was not always the case however as the name didn't stick in everybody's mind.

We were due to play at the Halfway House in Dunstable with Paper Lace, before their glory days of *Billy Don't Be a Hero* and *The Night Chicago Died*. The venue was in the middle of the town and greeting our arrival was a large banner proclaiming:

THE HALFWAY HOUSE WELCOMES PAPER LACE AND THE BRAIN ROBINSON SHOWGROUP

The advertising we received in Dunstable was clearly too much for our roadie John who tended to take things very much to heart – just joking John. However, he left soon and in his place we were fortunate to gain the services of my brother Peter.

President Records had not taken up the option of a follow-up single to *Don't Cast Aside* so we decided to make our own demo and try to secure another recording contract elsewhere. We booked a studio and laid down two tracks, the Four Seasons *Walk like a Man* and the Turtles song *Elenore*.

* * *

Lyn and I had continued to see one another on the occasions I was not involved with the band. During that time our relationship was still nothing more than a friendship. Neither of us had given much thought as to what the future might hold or indeed, if we had a future together at all. Eventually however we did finally become engaged and a while later got married. We needed somewhere to live and bought a small terraced house in Hotblack Road.

An Australian band called Black Stump arrived in Norwich. Soon after, the band members, Glen, Eddie, Barry and John changed their name to Helios. Johnny Jones, who was the singer, told me that he was looking for somewhere to live and asked if he could bed down at mine for a day or two until he had sorted himself out. I explained to Lyn that it was purely a short term arrangement and she somewhat hesitantly agreed that he could stay. The day or two stretched into weeks, as Johnny seemed to be no further forward in finding himself any permanent accommodation.

We put him in a small box bedroom at the back of the house where he stayed up all hours of the night drinking coffee and writing songs – *Camelot* was one song in particular that I remember stood out above the others. John then booked some time at Radio Luxembourg's London studios to record some demos of his songs and asked if our band would play on them and put down some backing vocals. We agreed and went to London where we stayed up most of the night at our lodgings in Sussex Gardens rehearsing the songs for the next day.

At the recording session Nick, Mick and Pete, along with a couple of other musicians that John had invited, were busying themselves so I went for a wander on my own round the building. I entered a vacant studio and saw what looked to me like an organ. I approached the instrument and pressed the keys only to hear a muffled grinding noise. Lifting the lid I saw a mangled mass of tape. I closed the lid and walked out of the room.

When I returned to our studio friction had developed between Johnny Jones and some of the others. Johnny, in particular, had incurred the wrath of roadie Peter whom he had expected to act as his fetch and carry for the day. When the recording session was finally over a friendly studio hand escorted us to the main exit. He asked if we had enjoyed our time there and hoped that everything had gone well. As we passed the studio I had briefly visited earlier he pointed a finger.

'See that in there,' he said. 'That's a sound sampler called a Mellotron, the same as the Moody Blues used on *Nights in White Satin*. It's a wonderful piece of kit,' he added admiringly.

'Oh is it,' I replied not giving it a second glance.

We arrived back home in Norwich and Johnny Jones finally departed Hotblack Road a couple of days later.

7

With the majority of our bookings now being away from Norwich there were very few opportunities for us to play local gigs. The Club America in Norwich was one place which we enjoyed and we were popular with its customers. We built up a great friendship with the manager Vic Johnson, barmen Freddie Savage and Brian Girling and Pineapple, the Polynesian doorman. We also got to know some of the regulars, including Norwich City footballers, Duncan Forbes, Graham Paddon and Alan Black, who always ensured that there were match tickets waiting for us when Norwich were playing away in the same towns and cities where we might be performing.

Another of the Club America regulars was someone I shall simply refer to as J. He lived in a large country house near Norwich and liked the band enough to sometimes travel further afield to see us play. Once we got to know him better we found out his family owned a freight business and he was due to inherit a large sum of money on his twenty-first birthday.

There were now two offices looking after our bookings. Barry Tyler was considered to be our main agent and any work offered by Norwich Artistes had to be conducted via the Kings Lynn office. Our acetate demo had been touted around the London record companies and we received the news that the Major Minor label was interested in signing us.

***

Opportunity Knocks, the popular TV talent show, was coming to Norwich and auditions to find new acts for the programme were being held at the studios of Anglia Television. It was further announced that the host, Hughie Green himself, would be attending. At that time the national newspapers were rife with stories about how the show was rigged in favour of certain contestants. We applied and received confirmation that we were among the successful applicants to be auditioned.

On the day of the audition, in front of the programme's genial host without any thought of consequence, we decided to include a parody that Pete and I had written. It was sung to the tune of the Bachelor's hit recording *I Wouldn't Trade You for the World.*

All together now 1 2 3...

Yes we won on Hughie's show, twenty-five weeks in a row...
(Backing vocals) *Weeks in a row...*
We don't know who fixed it for us, the Sunday papers say they know...
(Backing vocals) *The Sunday papers say they know*

We sandwiched the sketch in-between our opening and closing numbers and that Saturday morning we left the studio soon after to travel to Nottingham where we were appearing that night. During the journey we talked about how well we thought the audition had gone and agreed that it was perhaps a bit cheeky to have included the Bachelors routine. However what was done was done and that was that.

Sunday came and went and early on Monday evening there was a knock on the door at Hotblack Road. I opened it to be greeted by a man in a dark suit. Looking over his shoulder I saw, parked outside in the street, a large black saloon with its driver sitting behind the wheel. The man at the door said that he had something important to discuss with me and I invited him in. He said that his visit was in connection with our

Opportunity Knocks audition and asked if I could gather the rest of the band together to meet him.

An hour later we were all seated opposite the two strangers in the lounge of a nearby pub. They told us that a recording of our audition had been seen in London and there was interest in us appearing on the show. They said that we would be offered a contract which would guarantee us a minimum of three wins on the show. There was also talk of a further TV appearance on *the Simon Dee Show,* a popular Saturday night television programme of its day. These appearances would have given us four continuous weeks of prime time TV exposure when we would be seen by millions of viewers.

Listening to what they had to say, the whole proposition sounded very exciting but we couldn't understand why it was all so mysterious. We were told that we would go to London to make some recordings but would not be allowed to tell anyone who we were – they even went as far as to say that the bass drum skin bearing our name would have to be removed in order to keep our identity concealed. They said that the contract we would sign would be for three years, for which we would each receive thirty pounds per week. At that time I was earning fourteen pounds a week from my office job and the offer of more than double that amount certainly sounded appealing.

We explained that we were due to meet Major Minor and about the offer of the recording contract with them. We asked if we could have more time to consider our options but time was something they were not prepared to allow us. They said that the contract had to be completed quickly and, after giving us just twenty-four hours to make our decision, they left.

After they had gone we stayed behind in the pub trying to make some sense of everything that we had just heard. A number of things went through our minds that night just to add to the confusion.

Two people had taken the trouble to drive all the way from London to see us. Why would they do that if their offer was not genuine? Who were they? They had obviously seen our audition tape to know about our name being on the drum skin and they must have had access to our application form to know so much about us – how else could they have known where I lived? They hadn't given us any information about who we would be signing with and three years was a long time to be tied to a contract if it all went wrong. But why should it go wrong? They had talked about us making recordings. With the amount of television exposure they said we would receive there would surely be a record release and, who knows, maybe a hit record at that?

The thought of committing ourselves into signing a three year contract was of great concern. There had been no mention of any get-out clause if it didn't work out. Thirty pounds a week may have seemed a lot of money then but surely that would need to increase after a period of time? We had not been advised of any increase and three years later, with possibly a hit record or records to our name, thirty pounds a week would not have been such a good deal. A few years later it was reputed that an act, who had enjoyed considerable success on *Opportunity Knocks,* was earning a low and fixed amount whilst their record was number one in the charts. Could this have been the same deal as the one we had just been offered?

We considered it ironic that our Bachelors routine at the audition might well prove a prophecy of our impending situation? The more we talked about it the more intense became the discussion. Roger finally broke the tension by jokingly adding that the offer had to be genuine as our visitors had gone to the expense of paying for both rounds of drinks and a packet of cigarettes for us in the bargain!

I made late night calls to Barry Tyler and Colin our accountant. I told them what had taken place and an urgent meeting was arranged.

The following day we all met up and we related to Barry and Colin the events of the previous night. They listened and were both of the same opinion that we should not accept the offer. They were wary of the fact that the whole business had been conducted in such a secretive manner and why it needed to be concluded so quickly.

Barry said that the entertainment business was rife with unscrupulous people who had tied acts up with agreements that they could not get out of and how such agreements had actually destroyed careers. He mentioned one particular major star that had enjoyed considerable record success only to be cheated out of a fortune in royalties.

Accountant Colin came up with the possibility of future tax implications that could arise from such underhand dealings. Barry Tyler concluded the meeting by reminding us of our bright future, with plenty of work in the diary and a recording contract with Major Minor on the table.

'It's much better to know who you are dealing with,' he said.

That night the expected telephone call arrived and I gave our decision. There was no attempt from the other party to try and persuade us to change our minds. We will never know what might have happened had we decided to accept the proposal. On the rare occasions since then, when we have looked back, the subject of *Opportunity Knocks* has been mentioned. We have all been of the same opinion that, had we had our time over again and the same deal been offered to us, we would have taken it.

8

J turned twenty one. By now he had become a close friend and he spent more and more time in our company. He travelled to several of the places where we worked and sometimes acted as an additional roadie to Peter. As our friendship with J grew, so the venue for our practice nights upgraded from the local pub to the music room at his home.

His family were somewhat eccentric. J had a younger brother who took great delight in hurling tennis balls along the corridors of their country house. He would then watch the Labradors, in mad pursuit, slide frantically on the slippery wooden floors. There was also a pilot who appeared on the scene from time to time. I believe he may have been associated with the family business and it was said that he liked his drink – there were certainly occasions when he seemed to have had one too many.

The house itself was an imposing old building and surrounded by a moat. It even had its own ghost, a poltergeist, said by J's mother to be that of a young child who had died there. Whilst watching television one night the screen suddenly became a snowstorm.

'That will be you know who,' J's mother casually remarked and an investigation into one of the attic rooms revealed that the television aerial had been turned upside down. Another time, when we were practicing in the music room, a picture ejected itself from the wall and flew across the room.

'Okay so you don't like the song!' somebody in our party exclaimed to our mischievous friend.

From the time that he received his inheritance, J's generosity knew no bounds.

'We should have some new microphones,' he said one day, the 'we' seemingly binding him to the group. Five top of the range Shure mics were duly purchased followed shortly by Fender guitars for Nick and Mick and a Ludwig drum kit for Pete.

We were booked at Walton-on-the-Naze in Essex and only a few miles into the journey, with J following behind as usual in his Ford Mustang, roadie Peter's van broke down. Despite his efforts to get the van started it remained stubbornly immobile. We managed to contact the venue and explain what had happened. The owner said he was expecting a full house that night and asked us to get there any way possible. Eventually, and with no other alternative, he arranged for a van to collect the equipment and those of us able to squeeze into the remaining space. J took the rest in his Mustang. We arrived at the venue, albeit later than expected, but we completed the booking and had a good night.

At the end of the evening the proprietor refused to pay us saying that he'd had to cover the van expense in coming to pick us up and that we had played for less than our contracted time. Despite our protests he refused to budge from his decision and furthermore he insisted that we remove our equipment from his premises.

'But where are we going to go?' we pleaded when everything had been taken outside.

'Not my problem,' he replied as he bolted the front door.

We found ourselves in the car park on a windy sea front when J came up with an idea. He drove some of us the seventy-five miles back to Norwich before returning to his home and exchanging the Mustang for a Land Rover. He then travelled back to Walton where the remaining members had assembled the equipment into a shelter in order to gain protection from the blustery night conditions.

It was mid-morning on Sunday before everyone had arrived safely back in Norwich. Whatever happened to the van? Did Peter ever manage to get it started or maybe it is still there, abandoned behind the Magpie Inn in Stonham Parva?

'We need a new van,' J announced following the Walton-on-the-Naze debacle. We were surprised that the venue actually had the cheek to make an approach for another booking as people had apparently asked for us back. Needless to say the offer was politely declined.

A long wheel base Mercedes van was ordered from Park Royal in North London and it was then specially customised with all the equipment and requirements for the comfort and needs of a band on the road. When the customisation was complete it looked nothing like the original vehicle – it now had side windows, coach seats, sleeping quarters, an oven and a sink together with a partitioned area at the back to house the musical instruments. Our Mercedes ended up being something quite special and it was the envy of many a band that we came across.

We were now travelling further afield and often not getting back home until the early hours of the morning. We had talked about turning professional and the discussions were now becoming more frequent. We knew that making such a move would open up more opportunities of work across the country.

We had our recording date for Major Minor in the diary, each of us with our own burning ambitions; it was inevitable that we would eventually make the decision to quit our day jobs. We informed Barry Tyler and Phil Beevis and knew that, if we were to sustain any sort of living as a professional band, we would need all the bookings that they could come up with.

9

'See you later Ron,' I said.

It had just gone two in the afternoon and we had finished our lunchtime drinks. Ron was a work colleague; at least he had been until yesterday.

The previous day had been my final one at work. Today I had slept in and woke up with a sense of newly found freedom. Lyn had already left for work and I had nothing more to do other than decide how I would spend my day.

I did what I had always done during my working week. I went to the Wild Man pub and met up with Ron for our lunchtime drink. The difference now was that it was time for Ron to go back to work whereas I was free to do as I pleased.

**

One of our very early engagements as a professional band took place at Rebecca's nightclub in the centre of Birmingham. We were booked there for three nights and on the first night we appeared alongside the legendary American blues singer Chester Burnett, better known as Howlin' Wolf. During the afternoon sound-check, he showed an interest in Nick's Fender Telecaster guitar and asked if he could play it. Wolf was a very large and imposing man and, hunched over Nick's instrument, his body practically enveloped the guitar as he gave us a private rendition of his classic song *Smokestack Lightning*.

The following two nights we worked alongside the resident disc jockey. The DJ had clearly taken a shine to roadie Peter and at the end of Friday night he invited us all back to his home to stay the night. Peter had with him a tent which he sometimes slept in when the weather was kind and that night he decided to pitch it in the DJ's garden whilst the rest of us remained in the house. During the night I was awoken by Peter scurrying into the room.

'He's queer!' Peter exclaimed. Apparently the DJ had made an attempt to join him inside the tent.

'You mean you didn't know?' I said.

'No one told me,' he replied. Despite the obvious attention that he had received from the DJ earlier Peter didn't have an inkling about something that had been quite obvious to the rest of us.

On Saturday evening we returned to Rebecca's for our final session and, as we walked in, the DJ blew Peter a kiss. It seemed rather appropriate that the White Plains song *I've Got You on My Mind* was playing in the background.

* * *

Prior to our actual recording, we had a meeting with Major Minor's producer Dave Bernstein and musical director Nicky Welsh. They gave us four demo songs to take away and learn. The numbers we were given were *You Are All I Need*, *12:29*, *Scandinavian Blonde* and *Call My Name*. When we returned for the recording session Nicky Welsh was surprised how well Nick MacCartney had worked out the vocal harmonies.

'I thought you might have struggled with picking those out,' he remarked on two in particular.

Dave Bernstein next raised the subject of our name and said that he felt something more appealing to a record buying public was needed. We had been happy with the Brian Russell Showcase as it suited the type of cabaret work that we had been doing but we understood why such a change had to be made. Dave suggested that Edentree would be a better choice. We had an initial concern as there was already an established band called East of Eden on the scene but we eventually ended up in agreement and from that moment we became Edentree.

From Major Minor's offices in Great Marlborough Street, we then walked the short distance to Carnaby Street, the iconic thoroughfare of fashion during the sixties and seventies. A photographic session had been booked to promote the record and, for our new image, we selected a variety of frilly silk shirts and velvet trousers. The clothes were in garish colours and very much in keeping with what mod bands were wearing at that time.

During the afternoon we went to the recording studios where session musicians were already in the process of laying down the backing tracks of the songs we had been given. We were fortunate to have on that session some of the finest musicians in the country. Clem Cattini was on drums with Barry Morgan providing the extra percussion. Herbie Flowers played bass, Jim Sullivan guitar and Harry Stonham was the keyboard virtuoso. Clem had been a former member of chart-topping group the Tornados, Barry and Herbie went on to become members of Blue Mink and Big Jim Sullivan worked for many years with Tom Jones. Harry Stonham established himself as the musical director on a number of television shows dating back to the early Michael Parkinson programmes. Needless to say, with such a collection of musical talent, each track was recorded in virtually one take. We then went in and added the vocals. Of the four songs we had originally been given our personal favourite was *Scandinavian Blonde* but Major Minor decided on *You Are All I Need* as the A side and *Call My Name* the B.

* * *

J's spending was rapidly spiralling out of control. By now he had turned his attention to another band and they were also on the receiving end of his generosity with newly purchased musical equipment. He then met a woman upon whom he lavished all the love and financial affection he could muster.

He would take her out at night and whisk her on to the dance floor, gyrating like a man devoid of all inhibition.

J moved out of his home and into a property with his lady friend. He also rented another large house which virtually became a squat for people in the music business. His travels on the road with us became less frequent and we only met up with him on a few more occasions when we found ourselves back in Norwich.

Eventually J's seemingly bottomless pit of money dried up. In a short space of time he had inherited and lost a fortune.

10

Bookings to parts of the country where we had never previously been were coming in. Our first schedule, of an eight day run of clubs in the north-east of England, had been confirmed along with a number of two and three consecutive nights bookings in other parts of the country. There were also the one-nighters which involved hundreds of miles of travel. With so much time now being spent on the road, it had proven a sensible decision to have the Mercedes equipped with sleeping quarters. Peter's workload as our Road Manager was considerable. As well as being responsible for our transportation, together with the setting up and breaking down of the equipment, he was soon to have an additional role to play when he also became our sound engineer, and virtually the sixth member of the band.

* * *

There was great excitement on the day that *You Are All I Need* was released and we were pleased to hear it playing on the Club America juke box that evening when we appeared there. The club was packed to the rafters – we had played the venue many times before but that night it seemed as if Edentree had well and truly arrived. We went on stage for our first set dressed in our new Carnaby Street clothes.

'You can't get gear like that in Norwich,' some members of the audience remarked enviously to one another.

The green crushed velvet trousers that I was wearing were an extremely tight fit leaving very little to the imagination. On the upper floor of the Club America there was a balcony that overlooked the stage and dance floor. Owner Geoff Fisher and his wife Mary happened to be there watching when Mary made some giggly remark to a friend regarding my trousers. Geoff overheard the girly banter and, being the prude that he was; he took me to one side during our break and suggested that I change into something more respectable for our second spot.

I can remember the very first time that I heard our record played on the radio. My aunt Flo, who had taken a keen interest in the band's progress, called me excitedly at home one morning.

'Quick put the radio on,' she said. I switched on in time to catch the last few bars of *You Are All I Need*. We also heard it played on a few occasions whilst in the van travelling.

* * *

Our first eight day run of bookings in the north-east was almost upon us. We were to begin at Sunderland Comrades Club on a Sunday lunch-time followed by another venue that night. There were then a further six clubs throughout the week and we were scheduled to finish with lunchtime and evening shows on the following Sunday.

The day before we travelled north we appeared at RAF Bentwaters in Suffolk. It had gone 1.00 a.m. by the time we had packed everything away and we then made the three hundred mile trek to Sunderland, arriving on the outskirts of the city around breakfast time. The general lack of sleep during the journey, together with smoking too many cigarettes, had left some of us with tired and croaky voices.

The doors to the Comrades Club were open and we walked in to find staff already preparing for the lunchtime session. Cleaners were busying themselves wiping tables and vacuuming the carpet whilst the bar staff lined up half-filled beer glasses to help speed up the process of pulling pints once the doors to the public opened and the rush for service began.

By now we had developed a thirty-minute comedy routine which we usually featured during our first spot when audiences were more attentive. The second half was nearly all music. We completed the lunchtime session and in the evening Les Mack, the agent who had booked us, came to introduce himself saying that he had received good reports from the Comrades Club. Those first eight days, working in that entertainment hot spot of the country passed very quickly and we had completed what was considered to have been a successful run. Edentree was an unknown name in the north-east and Les Mack was the first agent in that region to take a chance on us. We were grateful for his support and belief in us but there would later be bigger and more established agencies seeking our services.

* * *

We came across some colourful characters during our travels in those early days.

Charlie Dungy was the concert chairman or the compere as he preferred to be known, at Baldock working men's Club. Charlie was an amiable man with a smile and pleasantries for everyone he came across. He welcomed the audience to the evening's entertainment by sauntering onto the stage with a cheery 'Good evening. Dungy's the name – Charlie Dungy.' The musical intro to his opening number played in the background as he drifted nonchalantly over to a table and kissed the hand of a woman. His movements were timed to perfection and his opening lyrics to the song delivered on cue.

'Lovely lady – I'm falling madly ....'

It was oh so patronising but somehow it all worked beautifully.

The Andromeda Club in Colchester was the brainchild of Geoff Lewis, along with his partner Jimmy. The venue was themed in authentic Grecian style, as befitting its title, and was decorated with an abundance of objets d'art, including a sculpture of the Princess Andromeda herself together with various statues of naked Gods from Greek mythology. Geoff was a very flamboyant character, popular with his customers and the Andromeda attracted both a gay and straight clientele. We had some great nights there.

We appeared for a week at the First Floor Club in Ipswich with the outspoken Irish comedian, Dave Allen. The Manageress there was a Maltese lady called Maria who proved to be the perfect hostess. She was always smiling and friendly but could also show the business side of her character.

At the end of the week the band were packing away the equipment and I went to collect payment from Maria in her office. She gave me the money and as we left the office we walked through the casino. She asked me if I gambled and when I told her I did not she suggested that I might like to try. She said that the tables had been going through a particularly bad losing streak for most of the evening and I suddenly had this vision of going back to the band with a handsome profit on our earnings.

'Come,' she said. 'There is a space on that table over there. Maria will show you, yeh?'

A while later I met up with the others who were waiting inside the van.

'Where have you been?' they asked. 'We've been looking all over for you.'

I produced our money, minus the twenty pounds that I had lost in the casino.

'At one point I was almost twenty pounds up,' I remarked, trying to sound as upbeat as I could but it didn't work.

'Fucking great,' I heard someone in the back mutter as I climbed into the van.

11

Looking after the affairs of the Barry Lee Show was taking up more and more of Barry Tyler's time and we sensed the possibility of our own careers stagnating as a result of this. We therefore decided that it was in our best interests to leave ABC Management and place ourselves in the hands of Norwich Artistes.

The three biggest agencies in the north-east at that time were Beverley Artistes, based in South Shields, AIR in Spennymoor, and the Bailey Organisation, with their chain of prestigious nightclub work. During our run of bookings for Les Mack, we had caught the attention of AIR resulting in them taking us on for several weeks throughout the year. Colin Pearson and John Wray ran the agency and had excellent backup from Jean who handled all the office work. Spennymoor Variety Club, from where their business operated, was a large nightclub that had presented headline names such as Tom Jones, Shirley Bassey and Tommy Cooper.

It was common practice for the acts working for them to contact the office of AIR daily in order to find out where they were appearing that night. Occasionally there would be an addition to the schedule and we would be told to go to the Variety Club for an afternoon show. A miners strike in the north-east could result in clubs and pubs profiting from the extra daytime bar trade. All the acts that had received similar instructions to us would congregate in the dressing room – Little and Large was one act in particular that I remember also being summoned.

John Wray, as well as being the entertainment agent, was also the keyboard player who fronted the house band. There was a message above the dressing room door for all to see as they made their way to the stage:

"AT THE END OF YOUR ACT PLEASE DON'T THANK THE BAND FOR THEIR BACKING – IT BECOMES BORING EVERY NIGHT. WE KNOW WE ARE GOOD – AND WE NEVER FINISH WITH MY WAY."

My Way was a reference to the Frank Sinatra song that many vocal acts used to end their spot.

Inside the Variety Club was a very long bar that had pennies glued to the counter. There was also a table football machine that would sometimes play a part in AIR's daily business decisions. A difference of opinion between Colin and John might be settled by the result of a game of table football.

There was one time when we appeared there that happened to coincide with Roger Cooke's birthday and quite a few of the regulars remained inside the club after the evening's entertainment had finished. The drink was flowing and spirits were high when it was mentioned that John Wray had a couple of mini motorcycles called Monkey Bikes on the premises. I have been reliably informed by Pete Holmes, whose engineering knowledge is far superior to mine, that Monkey Bikes were small Honda's with tiny wheels and engines and being fully functional with lights, brakes and the like. Someone suggested having a ride on them and very quickly the chairs and tables were rearranged to form a racetrack. The Spennymoor Speedway Race Trials then began. There were lots of crashes, spills and club furniture scattered everywhere together with a great deal of alcohol consumption. All great fun – happy birthday Roger!

* * *

In the London area we appeared in various venues that included the larger and more popular music pubs. Two in particular that stand out were the Royal Standard in Walthamstow and the Green Man in Leytonstone.

At Walthamstow the manager came to us at the end of one evening.

'You are good boys,' he said. 'You always do well for us and you never play south of the river.'

His comments seemed to refer to a time that was coming to an end, when the Kray twins had controlled parts of London before their incarceration. The manager's referral to us not working south of the river related to the area of the city ruled by the Kray's biggest rivals, the Richardson gang. Maybe it had been assumed that we knew all about divided loyalties and had maintained our allegiance to east and north London. Gang warfare was something we knew nothing about, and we certainly had no intention of becoming involved with, so we remained dumb and kept our noses clean.

The Green Man at Leytonstone will be best remembered, or perhaps I should say not remembered, for a completely different reason. Amongst the audience that night were some of Pete Holmes old London mates who had turned up to lend their support. They were great company and after we had finished I went with them to someone's house where the drinking continued. A joint was rolled and passed around soon followed by another. The night turned into a blur and recollections of that evening remains almost non-existent.

I feel it necessary at this point to inform those of you who are tut-tutting, that my flirtation with smoking pot ended many years ago. In the words of 10CC, it was just a silly phase I was going through.

12

There were not many occasions when Edentree experienced failure but one time when it did happen was completely down to me.

We were booked at RAF Waddington in Lincolnshire in what we thought was the Sergeants Mess. When we arrived we found out that we were playing to the Corporals. The audience was much younger and more rowdy and under practically no supervision. Despite our earlier reservations, we found ourselves doing surprisingly well until I improvised with the comedy.

A part of our act included a send up of Jimi Hendrix which involved me pretending to play a guitar with my mouth Hendrix-style before spitting out grains of rice to create the impression that the guitar strings had broken my teeth.

Whilst driving to Lincolnshire earlier that day, the news had come on the radio that Jimi Hendrix had died in London of a suspected heart attack. Hours later that night on stage at RAF Waddington the unexpected was about to happen.

To the guitar introduction of the song *Purple Haze,* I made my usual entrance donned in my afro wig and guitar in hand. This received an appreciative response from the audience but then, in a moment of spontaneity, I decided to change the routine. I promptly threw myself on the floor clutching my chest and simulating a heart attack. The crowd no longer saw the funny side and suddenly became incensed. They turned ugly against us as my improvisation well and truly backfired. We somehow managed to escape unscathed that night and during the journey home I made a mental note to give more thought and consideration to possible consequences before any future adlibs.

* * *

Another of Edentree's ten day runs in the north-east came around. By now we had become more established up there and, as well as the social clubs, we found ourselves booked for additional late-spots in nightclubs. After finishing at a working men's club we would rush off for a midnight cabaret at a number of venues that had sprung up in the area. There were Wetherells, the first of the Bailey clubs, La Strada and Annabel's in Sunderland, the Domino at Bedlington, the Senate at Peterlee, Darlington's Flamingo, La Ronde at Billingham, the Birdcage in Newcastle and Stockton Fiesta, perhaps the most celebrated of all. To work those types of places the acts were expected to be of a much higher calibre, an expectation openly manifested by the greeting received at our first appearance at Annabel's, 'You'd better be good because we've got a great house band here.'

That particular house band was led by keyboard player John Miles, who went on to achieve success with his record *Music*. No pressure then!

Sunday lunchtime in the north was a social institution. The clubs were mainly full of men, who sat in the same seats, and at the same table, whilst drinking the same brand of beer and each reading an identical copy of the same newspaper. I once asked why they didn't just buy different newspapers that could be swopped around. My question was met with incredulous glares. It seemed to be a ritual that, after the lunchtime session had ended, all the men returned home armed with their very own copy of the *News of the World* for their wives to read.

A screen of *News of the World* papers could go up and act as a barrier between the drinking customers and the stage if the performer was not capturing their attention. There was one particular act who became so frustrated with being ignored that, during the fire-throwing part of his second spot, he engulfed an entire row of newspapers in flames.

We were appearing at a club in County Durham on a typical Sunday lunchtime and seated together at two front tables was a group of lads, all drinking and playing bingo. The time came for our first spot and we opened with *Darlin'*. Towards the end of the set we performed another Beach Boys song, the haunting *In My Room*. It was during this song that I noticed one person from the group leave his seat to stand on his own at the side of the room listening. During our break he came across and introduced himself as Davey. He told us that he was a great fan of the Beach Boys and said how much he had enjoyed our spot, especially *In My Room,* which happened to be one of his favourite songs. Davey then introduced us to Big Arthur, another Davey and George. We ended our second spot with *Good Vibrations* and by now the bunch of lads were well and truly on our side. They asked where we were next playing as they wanted to come and see us again and we gave them our upcoming schedule of venues.

They were as good as their word and became our adopted fan club, regularly turning up whenever we were playing in the north-east. They were a good natured lot and we remained friends with some of them after Edentree had split up. Unfortunately Davey is no longer with us but, for a number of years after we had finished, George Hetherington kept in touch and occasionally travelled down to Norwich to spend a few days with us.

* * *

We made a number of other friends in the north-east and some of them invited us to stay with them at their homes whenever we were in the area.

Keith and Christine were from Chester-le-Street. Keith was affectionately known as "The Netty Man," "Netty" is Geordie slang for toilet and the nickname derived from what he did to earn a living. Sometimes Keith would come with us and assist Peter with the roadie duties.

There were also John and Eileen who lived in Hartlepool. John was a southerner, a considered foreigner and a great jazz fan. He would keep us up half the night playing music from his prized record collection. John was quite a suave character and always had that little bit of an "edge" about him.

John and Eileen had a friend called Jerry who was a colossus. He stood well over six feet tall and sported a Teddy-Boy style of jet black hair, scooped back and complete with long bushy sideburns. He was also the proud owner of one of the biggest beer bellies that I have ever seen. One Sunday I was with John and Eileen at their local pub when Jerry came in having just finished his morning shift at the abattoir where he worked. I asked if I could have a shower and he gave me a key to his bungalow just around the corner.

I was in the shower, and heavily lathered, when suddenly the shower curtain was yanked aside. Jerry had finished his pint and returned home to clean up. He was stripped naked and in all his glory. It was not a sight for the faint-hearted.

'Move over,' he said unperturbed by my presence.

Charlie and Margaret lived in Seaham Harbour, at that time no more than a small fishing and mining community on the east coast, just off the A19, a few miles south of Sunderland. It became a place that we got to know very well – roadie Peter took an interest in the local fishermen and their daily catch whilst Pete Holmes and I spent many an hour sitting by the harbour trying to think up new ideas for the act.

I was staying with Charlie and Margaret one night and was asleep on their couch. They had been out late drinking and I was abruptly awoken by the sound of their back door being flung open. In rushed Margaret screaming. The couch I was on happened to be near the bottom of their staircase and, without breaking her stride, Margaret scrambled over me and rapidly disappeared up the stairs. Charlie followed in hot pursuit, waving in the dark what appeared to be a chopper. He followed the same route as Margaret over my reposed body. From upstairs came the sound of a great deal of shouting and swearing and I listened intently until it eventually became quiet again and I drifted back to sleep.

Next day the couple had returned to their normal selves and it was as if the events of the previous night had never taken place. I knew that they were prone to having heated rows ...but with a chopper?!

This story soon spread through Seaham Harbour and, after a certain amount of embellishment by almost everyone who relayed the tale, Charlie then became known locally as "The Axe Man."

13

In July 1970 the BBC Radio One Roadshow came to the Norwich Lads Club. A series of those midweek shows took place in different towns and cities throughout the summer months. The show was fronted by a BBC disc jockey and its two-hour format was a mixture of playing records, prize give-aways and interviews together with an appearance by a guest band. The programme went out live to the nation at twelve noon.

The guest DJ for Norwich happened to be Tom Edwards, a popular choice due to his local media connections. The New Seekers had been booked for an interview and we were offered the live band slot. We agreed to take part even though it meant an overnight drive from our previous night's booking – in order to be at the venue for 8.00 a.m. the next morning.

It was the first time that I had been back at the Lads Club since my footballing days in 1963. The venue itself was a typical sports hall and was acoustically poor. It was originally built for the purposes of boxing, table tennis and football events and was most certainly not the ideal place to stage live music.

During our early morning sound-check the echo, enhanced by an empty hall, meant that we had great difficulty controlling the whistles of feedback from our PA system whenever we tried to increase the volume. The BBC microphones were taped to our own and our vocals were then fed to a sound engineer in a trailer outside in the car park.

'It should be okay once we get bodies in to soak up the sound,' the producer unconvincingly assured us after hearing the screeching feedback.

The songs we were to perform had to be logged and we gave him our running order – *C'mon Marianne* by the Four Seasons and *Ride My See Saw* by the Moody Blues in the first set and *Carpet Man* by Fifth Dimension finishing with *Good Vibrations* by the Beach Boys in the second.

'Are you sure about *Good Vibrations*? It's a bit of a complicated number,' the producer asked, as if he considered that we were incapable of doing 'complicated'.

He was indeed correct about the song being a very complex piece of work. I had witnessed the Beach Boys themselves make a hash of it only a few months earlier. On that particular night however I had made allowances for the fact that it happened to be Dennis Wilson's birthday. Perhaps one celebratory drink too many may have been a contributing factor as to why he had wobbled precariously on his drum stool during the number *I Get Around*.

We assured the producer that we didn't have a problem with the song.

'Well if you're sure,' he said before turning and heading off in another direction when someone said that Tom Edwards had just arrived.

Midday came and the Radio One Roadshow was live. The feedback we had experienced earlier was just as persistent despite the presence of the bodies that were supposed to soak up the sound. As a last desperate measure, we pushed our PA speakers as far possible to the front of the stage as we could whilst we performed behind them. With no monitor system for us to hear, and surrounded by the combined noises of the drums and guitar amps, we became immersed in a wall of sound. I have a reel to reel copy of the broadcast tape and the sound balance is not up to the standard that it should have been, possibly due to the fact that the engineer was mixing blind outside in the trailer. During the four numbers we were constantly changing our individual vocal roles, which ranged from singing lead one minute to backing harmony the next. If the engineer had been able to identify who was doing what, and when, the final result would probably have been a lot better.

After the Roadshow, the BBC however seemed to have been impressed enough to ask us to record a number of tracks to be used as inserts in their daily radio pop programmes.

***

Major Minor had gone very quiet. There were a few more occasions when *You Are All I Need* was heard on the radio but it was obvious now that whatever chance the record might have had of success had gone. The option of extending our contract with them was never taken up, which we were disappointed with because we considered that *Scandinavian Blonde*, the intended follow-up single, was a much catchier number.

I can't give a reason or indeed any precise account of what actually went wrong with Major Minor. What is clear however is that at some point there had been discussions as to how the record was to be promoted. It was whispered common knowledge that there were fixers in the business who could arrange extensive radio and media coverage in exchange for money. J is believed to have offered to put up five thousand pounds for a vested interest in *You Are All I Need*.

I was not present when any such discussions might or might not have taken place but I do recall some time later there were people asking where the money had gone as it had not been forthcoming as promised.

14

We played for three nights at the Merrion Centre in Leeds. The nightclub was called Stringfellows and named after its owner. The venue had two round podiums on the edge of a large dance floor and we were set up on one with Peter Stringfellow opposite on the other. DJ Peter had long bleached blonde hair and he wore a white suit, virtually the same image that he portrayed throughout his later and more illustrious career. He played a good mixture of music, including some American imports long before they were released in the UK.

When we had first turned professional we vowed that we would devote as much of our spare time as possible to learning new material and working to improve the act. Unfortunately the number of hours that we spent on the road travelling made this very difficult. Sometimes we could only gain access to a venue an hour or so before they opened so the best opportunities for rehearsals were when we were booked into the same place on consecutive nights and our equipment could be left in place. The three nights at Stringfellows were therefore ideal and on Thursday, after we'd had a good opening night to an appreciative audience, we asked Peter if we could use the club the following day.

Peter Stringfellow was a showman who had mastered the art of creating a party atmosphere on the dance floor. One of the records he played, and which received a good audience response, sounded very much like a number called *Candida* which was in our repertoire. We discovered that the record Peter played was *Knock Three Times*, already a big success in the US and due for release soon in Britain as Dawn's follow up single to *Candida*. We asked if we could borrow the record to learn. The song was not difficult and we got it off very quickly. During the second night, and with the benefit of another good crowd, we felt confident enough to perform it live for the first time.

'Not bad,' said the ever critical Nick MacCartney afterwards. 'It will get better.'

* * *

We were seeing very little of home which was not exactly conducive to a happy married life. We'd complete a run of dates, travel back to Norwich and soon after we would be off again. Sometimes our home visits were nothing more than a glorified stop off for a change of clothing. There were occasions when Lyn was waking up as I arrived back in the early hours of the morning and I would be gone again by the time she returned from work that night. Mick and I were both married to wives who had jobs to fill their day and neither of us at that time had children. It was particularly difficult for Pete Holmes who had a wife and two young sons to take care of.

* * *

Nowadays, Recreation Vehicle travel is a popular pastime enjoyed by millions throughout the world. People take to the roads in luxurious motor homes that are equipped with every conceivable mod-con you can imagine.

With all the amenities for comfortable living that we had installed in our Mercedes we might well have been considered pioneers of RV travel. During the warm weather we sometimes followed roadie Peter's lead and slept in tents when conditions allowed. We thus began to lead an almost Bohemian lifestyle as we became adept at setting up camp in the early hours of the morning. Sometimes it was foggy after a warm day and come daylight we would emerge bleary-eyed from our tents to find that we had camped on a grass verge next to a motorway or, on one occasion, on the front lawn of a very classy looking country house just outside Birmingham. That property had gushing fountains with stone steps leading up to a grand entrance and we awoke to a very concerned Lord and Lady of the manor peering at us through the curtains.

One of our impromptu camp sites was near Dunstable. One particular week we were working one-nighters in the Hertfordshire area and, rather than drive home each night, we found ourselves a secluded field and decided to pitch camp. Roadie Peter could conjure up a great meal from some very basic ingredients and there was a river nearby which satisfied his great passion of fishing. That week we were blessed with warm weather, good food and little else to do but eat and sleep in between getting ready for a show somewhere.

The constant travelling was a necessary evil sometimes made much worse when our destinations did not follow any geographical order. In was not unusual to find ourselves covering a thousand miles or more in a week. We would sometimes head north to Newcastle on the A1 and considered ourselves fortunate if our bookings were confined to the surrounding districts of Sunderland, Gateshead, Middlesborough and South Shields. Sometimes we weren't quite so lucky and we might find ourselves in Newcastle one night, somewhere in the Midlands the next, and then back to Hartlepool before moving on to Bristol or Manchester and so on. The travelling became tedious and we each had our own way of coping with the boredom.

Roadie Peter did most of the driving as he had an incredible constitution and could stay awake for hours at a time. Nick was our map navigator; there were no SatNavs or mobile phones in those days. Roger used to sing a lot whilst Mick sat next to Nick in the front and generally took the mickey out of everybody and everything. Pete Holmes and I usually occupied the back seats and continued our endeavours to come up with new ideas for the act. In between we slept.

When we were awake we would think of different ways of passing the time. On one particular long journey during a very hot and glorious summer's day we found it more comfortable to discard some of our clothing in order to keep cool. Our shirts, first to be removed, were followed by shoes and socks and next off came our trousers. Great amusement followed when someone removed his underpants and placed them on his head. Soon all of us, except roadie Peter, were sitting completely naked with our pants on our heads creased up with laughter. We were shortly aware of the van slowing down and then coming to a halt, discovering that Peter had created a traffic jam by driving down the middle of a very busy and narrow street market. People were flocking around our van and peering through the windows giving us the sort of public exposure that we could have done without!

**

Those warm summer days occasionally caused me problems – I suffered from hay fever and took antihistamine tablets to help ease the discomfort of itchy eyes and sneezing.

It was a Saturday, and the last day of yet another trip to the north-east. It was also going to be a hectic day – we were booked into a social club in Seaton Carew for both the lunchtime and evening sessions prior to ending up later that night with a midnight cabaret spot at the Carousel nightclub in Chester-le-Street. George, Davey and Big Arthur turned up in a minibus with some of their other mates for our lunchtime spot. As they were all staying on for the evening we decided to spend the afternoon having a game of football in a nearby field.

The club bar had remained open during the afternoon. George and company had enormous capacities for drinking beer. I struggled to keep up with them, eventually conceding defeat and switching to whisky. The afternoon grew hotter and the drinks kept coming. I began to feel feverish and was constantly sneezing so I swallowed more antihistamine tablets in an attempt to try and try and gain some relief.

Whilst we were on stage for our first spot that night I felt quite unwell. It was later, whilst we were getting ready to continue on to the Carousel, that I passed out.

I am told what followed began with me regaining consciousness and acting very aggressively. The others realised that something was wrong and an ambulance was called. I can vaguely remember someone holding my arms and trying to restrain me before I was sedated.

When I opened my eyes a clock, staring at me from an opposite wall, announced that it was 3.00 a.m. A nurse was hovering above me trying to insert a rubber tube into my mouth. I gagged and fought against it but I was held firm and eventually offered little more resistance.

'Just relax your throat and swallow,' the nurse demanded.

The tubing was then fed down into my stomach and a funnel connected to the end of the tube. A warm soapy liquid was poured into the funnel. When the stomach pumping was finally over I was taken to a ward where my brother Peter was waiting. He had come with me in the ambulance to the hospital while the others had gone on to complete our booking at the Carousel. As well as the paramedics, the police had also been called. They suspected that I had been taking drugs and insisted on searching my bags but nothing was found. They left without charging me after Peter had explained about the amount of alcohol I had consumed whilst overdosing on hay fever tablets.

I was discharged from Sunderland hospital the next morning and we made the long journey back to Norwich by train where Lyn was waiting at the station. After the previous night's experience I had dark circles under my eyes and a gaunt and hollow look. There was no sympathy from Lyn, not that I was expecting or deserved any.

15

We travelled to London for our recording date with the BBC. The session took place at their Paris Studios in Lower Regent Street and we laid down six tracks which were later inserted into their various Radio One programmes. It gave our spirits a lift when we heard our songs played – on one occasion the fade-out of a number was followed by the familiar tones of presenter Jimmy Young with 'And oft you jolly well go you Edentree you.' We were grateful for the airtime, which gave us a bit of national exposure and helped to keep our name in the public eye.

* * *

We played to the residents of Norwich Prison where we literally had a captive audience. Permission had been granted for us to take along a go-go dancer. Lulu's scantily-clad appearance certainly added spice to the occasion and no doubt gave the inmates something different to think about that night. After we had finished playing the "Red Bands", a group of privileged prisoners, helped us with pack away our equipment and we were allowed to reward them with cigarettes.

Mick Elliott's father-in-law was a prison officer at a women's open prison in Sutton Valance in Kent. East Sutton Park was a Grade II-listed 15th Century mansion and housed about ninety prisoners. It was a fairly low grade place of reform used during the final stages of sentencing before release. The female prisoners arranged their own visits of family and friends on their Open Days and we appeared at one of those occasions.

From Kent, and in complete contrast, we then played a gay bar at Ashton-in-Makerfield in Lancashire followed by an appearance at the legendary Wigan Casino, where Northern Soul music began. We then journeyed the short distance from Wigan to Liverpool's Pyramid Club.

We were booked for two nights at the Pyramid and when it was over I went to the manager's office to get paid.

'It's ten pounds short,' I said after the money had been counted into my hand.

'That's what I have been told to pay you,' the manager replied despite my showing him the agreed amount in the contract. We continued to argue the point until I'd had enough and insisted on speaking with the owner.

The manager dialled a number before handing me the phone and a gruff voice at the other end answered. I explained what had happened and when the gruff voice refused to accept that we had been underpaid I voiced a torrent of anger down the line and suggested that he got off his fat arse and came to the club to sort the matter.

'Do you know who that was?' asked the manager after the phone had been replaced on its cradle. 'That was Brian London.'

I had heard of Brian London and remembered him as being a former British Heavyweight boxing champion. I suddenly had this vision of him indeed getting off his fat arse and coming to the club to sort the matter, and probably me in the bargain. I decided that a dispute over ten pounds was not worth an altercation with someone who had twice fought for the World Heavyweight boxing title.

Later, after I could find no evidence whatsoever of Brian London's involvement with the Pyramid Club, I realised I had been a victim of the wicked scouse sense of humour.

We turned up at Sheffield City Hall only to discover that the event was a student night and furthermore we were appearing with the Move and Atomic Rooster. We were angry at what we felt was a totally inappropriate booking on our agent's part but we were there and had little choice other than prepare ourselves to face the proverbial death.

We sorted a playlist of songs that we felt might just give us a chance of getting by with the younger and rock influenced audience. The playlist included a version of Free's *All Right Now*. Although we had never actually learnt the song we knew the basics of the number and, when we did occasionally perform it, I managed to drag it out by adlibbing all manner of lyrics and phrasing. The band, not knowing what was coming next, then did their best to follow me which meant that the arrangement was unpredictable to say the least. I don't suppose that we ever performed it the same way twice but it worked and on a good night *All Right Now* could last for anything up to ten minutes.

We were first on to the packed hall of students. The adrenalin kicked in and we were flying. We pulled out all the stops and got away with it, receiving a tremendous response at the end of our set.

* * *

The constant travelling had become routine. Occasionally the monotony of the one-nighters away was broken when we got to play venues in Norfolk. Ted Hardwick's Tower nightclub in Great Yarmouth for a week long engagement together with a mini summer season for Daisy West at a Caister-on-Sea holiday park and Gorleston's Polynesian Club were blessings and enabled us to put down some roots for at least a short while before we were on the move again.

There was a Christmas when we were booked for a hotel in Melrose on the Scottish border. We had accepted the booking on the understanding that we could bring our families and, after spending three days of that festive season together, we parted company with them somewhere along the A1. They continued their journey back to Norfolk whilst we diverted and made our way to York.

A few months later we were down south during the warmer summer climes.

This trip included a week at Penelope's nightclub in Paignton followed by a memorable night at Kings Country Park in Canvey Island, where the owner was impressed enough with us to crack open a bottle of champagne in celebration. We said goodbye to Essex nursing headaches and travelled to Thornaby in North Yorkshire. Not long afterwards we found ourselves once again back south – this time at the Aquarius Club in Hastings and holiday parks in St Leonards-on-Sea and Winchelsea. We also played Nero's nightclub in Margate and then moved on to its sister club further along the coast at Ramsgate.

My brother Peter had proven himself to be an excellent asset to Edentree. As a roadie he climbed mountains of stairs with heavy speakers in each hand and a drum case strapped to his back but he contributed so much more. Added to his very capable cooking skills, he was mechanically knowledgeable and, along with Pete Holmes, ensured that our van was maintained in good running order. He also became a proficient tailor when he bought fabric and made himself a pair of trousers after being unable to find any with wide enough flares for his liking. He became our bodyguard on the night outside the Southbank Club in Middlesbrough where we had been appearing with the Drifters. We got ourselves into a bit of bother with some locals and Peter stood his ground, armed with a microphone stand in one hand and in the other a baseball bat nicknamed "The Skinhead Club," which he kept in the van for such situations, until the gang finally backed off.

* * *

Audiences and northern audiences in particular, could be a very demanding lot. As a five-piece band Edentree generally found it easy to make a connection with the public but it could sometimes be a daunting task for the acts who failed to live up to expectations. The north boasted some of the finest night-clubs in the country offering the biggest names of the day. A northern audience would soon let you know if they thought you were not good enough. It was unwise to ever underestimate the power of an audience – they were capable of elevating you to an almost Godly-like status one minute but then bring you down to earth with a bump the next.

We certainly experienced the former in County Durham, where a club in Newton Aycliffe had not long been built and was one of the largest in the area. We had gone down well when we played there on a couple of previous occasions and when we arrived for our third visit we discovered it was an all ticket affair with a SOLD OUT sign on a display board outside.

That night we made our entrance to loud whistles and cheers and could do no wrong. Everything we did was greeted with raucous laughter and thunderous approval. The evening just got better and better and after our final number the applause was so loud it felt as if the roof was about to cave in. The reaction we received that night in Newton Aycliffe was as good as any I believe Edentree ever experienced.

An audience could also be unforgiving and soon after our Newton Aycliffe triumph we appeared in Northumberland at Newbeggin-by-the-Sea. During the evening the crowd had virtually ignored us and, with little more than twenty minutes before the end, Mick's amplifier decided to pack up. He plugged into Nick's which had also started to make strange spluttering noises. We managed to get through our final number when the little or no reaction we had received all night suddenly turned to cheers. The concert chairman put his head round the dressing room door.

'Come back lads,' he said. 'They're shouting for more.'

We tried to explain to him about the problems with the equipment.

'You mean you're not coming back on?' he said aghast.

'We're sorry but....' and without allowing any further explanation from us he left the dressing room and returned to his microphone.

'Ladies and gentlemen,' he announced. 'I have asked the band to come back for another number but they have refused.' The cheers immediately turned to boos.

When everything had finally quietened down the concert chairman returned to the dressing room.

'Here's your money,' he uttered tossing an envelope onto the table.

'Edentree,' he exclaimed. 'Eden fucking wank!'

16

I was back in Norwich and sitting in the office of Norwich Artistes.

'There are a couple of guys coming to see you Wednesday,' informed Phil, lighting yet another cigarette.

'Okay,' I said. 'Who are they?'

'Chinn and Chapman,' he replied.

* * *

Chinn and Chapman came from two completely different backgrounds. Nicky Chinn's family were affluent and owned successful businesses. Nicky had already tasted success as a songwriter in 1970 when he co-wrote with Mike d'Abo the two main songs for the film *There's a Girl in My Soup*. Australian born Mike Chapman was a professional musician and songwriter with the band Tangerine Peel as well as being a part-time waiter at a nightclub that Chinn used to visit. It was there the two met and decided to team up as songwriters forming an association with Mickie Most's RAK Label.

Chinn and Chapman had enjoyed a moderate chart success with a song called *Funny Funny* by a band called Sweet and they were on the lookout for new talent. They turned up on a wet and windy Wednesday night at an American air base in Suffolk where we were playing. The weather had done us no favours and the club was practically empty.

During our first spot we noticed two people sitting at a table halfway down the room and guessed it to be them. With hardly anybody in we had very little opportunity of creating any kind of atmosphere and when we finished our set the couple came across and introduced themselves. Nicky Chinn and Mike Chapman said they had liked what they heard and asked a few questions about the band. Following some small talk about the weather and the lack of people in the audience they bid their farewells and left.

Not long after that Phil told me that Chinn and Chapman wanted to see us in London. We met up with them at Nicky Chinn's sumptuous apartment off Park Lane and they told us that they were interested in recording us. Mike Chapman then handed us a demo disc.

'What's this?' we said and his never to be forgotten words came back at us.

'It's your first number one.'

The song was called *Chop Chop*, the tale of a Norwegian woodcutter. Mike Chapman had single-handedly played, sung and produced the demo and the thing that instantly grabbed us was the number's simplicity. Mike had played a twelve-string guitar and the percussion was nothing more than a nail clinking rhythmically between two milk bottles. We were given the demo to take away and learn.

The backing track had already been completed when we went into the studio a few weeks later to record the vocals. There was a great sense of disappointment listening to the finished version. We felt that *Chop Chop* had been heavily over-produced and had lost much of the appeal of Mike Chapman's original demo.

Sweet meanwhile followed up *Funny Funny* with another equally catchy title. *Co Co* was released and there were high expectations it would do well. The initial response to it however was slow, with the record making little impression on the charts.

* * *

Tony Blackburn was the BBC's golden DJ of the day. He had proven himself influential in promoting records; the public seemed to take notice of the music he played. Originally Tony had been associated with bubblegum and mainstream pop but he later turned his interest to soul music. It was largely thanks to his constant playing on the radio that a Diana Ross album track *I'm Still Waiting*, was released in the UK. as a single in 1971 and reached number one. As well as with being a DJ, Tony was a singer and had previous record releases to his name.

One morning I received a call from a friend asking if I'd seen the *Melody Maker*, a weekly music paper. I had not and he told me that, included in the new record releases for that week was *Chop Chop* by Tony Blackburn. I rang Norwich Artistes who didn't seem to know anything about it and after further investigation we discovered that Tony Blackburn's version of *Chop Chop* used the same backing track as the one on our recording but with his vocals replacing ours.

Soon after Sweet's *Co Co* received considerable radio play which had the desired effect and the record eventually went on to reach number two in the charts. Sweet had their second hit and Tony Blackburn had his recording contract.

We were never given an explanation by Chinn and Chapman as to what happened regarding our record and can only assume that it had been sacrificed for the success of *Co Co*. Our only consolation was that Tony Blackburn's *Chop Chop* never did become the number one success that Mike Chapman had so boldly predicted. Sweet later recorded a version of the song as an album track alongside a number called *Alexander Graham Bell*, which had been intended as our follow up single.

* * *

I look back on those times with Edentree and consider that we had brushed with national success on more than one occasion. I feel we had been unlucky with both our recording opportunities and that certain key decisions were taken out of our hands. I think that some of the influential people we had encountered along the way might well have offered us more than a fair chance of success had a little bit of good fortune gone our way. I accept that the *Opportunity Knocks* episode was entirely down to us valuing the opinion of other people instead of following our own instincts but I do believe that certain things happened with both Major Minor and Chinn and Chapman that we had little control over.

Chinn and Chapman eventually became the most prolific song writing team of the seventies. Following their success with Sweet, they wrote a string of hits for New World, Gary Glitter, Mud, Racey, Suzi Quatro and Smokie until their success in the UK was overtaken by Stock, Aitken and Waterman in the eighties. Mike Chapman then went on to become influential in moulding Blondie when he produced the band's hits *Heart of Glass*, *The Tide Is High*, *Sunday Girl*, *Atomic* and *Rapture*. Chinn and Chapman's song writing skills also earned them a number one hit in the US in 1982 with *Mickey* for Toni Basil.

* * *

The summer was coming to an end and future bookings for Edentree were beginning to fill the diary. We would soon be returning to familiar places where familiar faces would be turning out to greet us. I suddenly realised that, for the first time since we had been together, there were no fresh challenges to look forward to and with nothing new on the horizon our performances felt stale and tedious. Travelling all over the country had become monotonous and, as strange as it may seem with the six of us constantly in each other's company, it was a somewhat lonely existence.

I knew that my heart wasn't in it anymore. All the drive and enthusiasm I had previously felt was no longer there and I knew that it was the right time for me to leave the band.

It was almost as if my intention had been anticipated because, at that same time, two of the others had the self-same decisions. Both Peters announced that they too were leaving and so we decided that RAF Coltishall, at the end of January 1972, was to be Edentree's final booking with its original line up.

When it finally came about, the parting of the ways with Edentree was amicable. Nick, Mick and Roger considered that there was still some mileage left in the name and recruited local drummer Barry Wortley. The four of them continued to work together for another three years. There was a time we talked about the possibility of me managing the new line up but that was as far as it got.

17

Norwich Artistes was recognised as very much an established and respected entertainment agency within the music industry thanks mainly to Phil Beevis. During my days off with Edentree I spent a great deal of my spare time helping out in their office and, in doing so, had gained what would later prove to be invaluable experience regarding the general running of the business.

Friction had developed between John and Phil and it came to a head when Phil was offered the chance of relocating to North Norfolk and booking the bands into West Runton Pavilion and Cromer Links, two very popular venues of the day. Phil seized the opportunity with both hands and proceeded to repeat his earlier success at the Melody Rooms. He helped swell the attendances at both venues by bringing in established bands such as the Who, the Move, Marmalade and the Tremeloes whilst also introducing new talent.

Thin Lizzy, Nazareth and Queen were just three bands whose stars were in the ascendancy when Phil booked them. Phil Beevis would later go on to form his own agency, Alert Entertainments.

After he had moved away from Norwich in 1972 I missed Phil's company a great deal. We'd had some good times together in the six years that we had known one another. Phil Beevis made an ever lasting impression on me and I am certain that, without his inspiration, I would not have gone on to enjoy over five decades in this business.

* * *

My Edentree days were now behind me and I had given little thought as to what my next move might be. I was unemployed when the departure of Phil Beevis left a gap in Norwich Artistes and I accepted John Fisher's offer of becoming Phil's replacement in the agency. The office was then still situated at Fisher's Freehouse in Prince of Wales Road but John's father, Geoffrey was entering into new business ventures.

He had taken over the Yare public house in Brundall and acquired South Walsham Hall, which he intended turning into a Country Club. In contrast, he offloaded some of his other businesses – the Miramar Cafe in White Lion Street had gone and Vic Johnson became the new owner of Club America. It was now the turn of Fisher's Freehouse to be sold.

With our office gone, Norwich Artistes needed new premises and John came up with the idea of buying a large residential caravan and placing it in the garden of his home at Lindley House. Phone lines were installed and the business was run from the caravan. I was now dealing with more of the day to day running of the office due to John combining his agency role with managing the Melody Rooms. I found my feet very quickly and was negotiating deals for headline names such as Sweet, Blackfoot Sue, Rory Gallagher, Slade and Status Quo. I was also looking after a number of local groups, some of whom I managed to book into venues in other parts of the country, thanks mainly to the contacts I had established during my time on the road.

One morning I arrived at Lindley House for work as usual only to discover an empty plot and the caravan suspended by a crane in mid-air. John had not considered the fact that he might need planning permission for the caravan to be used for commercial purposes and so we were on the move again, this time to an office in St Vedast Street.

* * *

The phone rang and I answered.

'Hello its Aubrey Gray,' a voice on the other end replied.

Aubrey owned a nightclub in Norwich called El Piana which was scheduled to reopen after refurbishment following a fire at the premises. It had a downstairs bar and restaurant together with another bar and function room upstairs. Aubrey told me that he intended to present cabaret six nights a week and was looking for a resident band. Phoenix was one of the bands I represented able to take on such a full time commitment and I took them to El Piana to audition for Aubrey. He heard them play and immediately wanted to book them.

'What are you up to?' he turned to me and asked. 'I will also need a compere.'

Since finishing with Edentree, I had not considered the idea of actually performing again but Aubrey's offer was appealing and so I agreed.

Backed by Phoenix, I opened the evening at El Piana with a song followed by some banter with the audience before introducing the band for their first set. There was then a short break with taped music playing followed by a visiting cabaret act and finishing up with a final set from Phoenix. The cabaret artistes arrived on a Sunday and performed six shows during the week with Wednesday being their night off.

Aubrey had also asked me to book the cabaret and I looked to my time with Edentree when we had worked with some excellent acts. I had also established a good working relationship with Mary Arnold, a London agent and the mother of actress Debbie Arnold. Mary's husband Maurice King personally managed the solo career of singer Scott Walker after the split of the Walker Brothers.

* * *

One of the first acts that I booked from Mary was a Welsh singer called Tammy Jones. I turned up at the El Piana for a Sunday afternoon to find Tammy waiting outside. She was sitting on a suitcase and had a plastic bag on her head to protect her from the rain. Tammy later went on to find success on *Opportunity Knocks* and followed that up with her big record success *Let Me Try Again*.

The acts I was coming up with ranged from the sublime to the plain ridiculous. There was a speciality duo consisting of a young West Indian male who juggled and performed limbo dancing and fire eating. He then stuck pins in himself and walked on flaming coals before finally laying bare back on broken glass while his older female partner stood on him.

I also booked a very rotund lady who turned out to sing rather badly, and most certainly would have died on her backside had it not been for her dog. On her opening night the pet Chihuahua remained in the dressing room until she had finished her final number which received a meagre response from the audience. At this point the small canine raced out and leapt into the arms of "The Large Lady." The audience mouthed a few appreciative 'Ahhhs,' and there followed a ripple of applause from a few animal lovers.

The following night her performance had once again reached its anticlimax but this time the Chihuahua did not make an appearance. The dressing room door had been accidently closed thus preventing the show saving rescue.

Her week went from bad to worse when Phoenix and I were having an afternoon rehearsal and I just so happened to be wearing her dress, doing a more than passable impression of her, when she unexpectedly walked in.

'I expect you're wondering what I'm doing in this?' I mumbled as I slipped her garment from my shoulders.

They say that revenge is sweet and "The Large Lady" certainly got that on her final night when I walked into the dressing room barefoot and promptly stood in a bowl of soft squelchy dog food.

Charlie Lee was a likeable comedian from Liverpool and had a face that you felt you knew. And you could be right because it seemed that whenever there was press coverage of any kind, Charlie could always be found lurking in the background, peering over someone's shoulder and beaming into the camera. He loved the limelight and had the knack of being in the right place at the right time.

There is a lovely story about Charlie Lee gate-crashing a Frank Sinatra concert at the Royal Festival Hall in London during 1971. Charlie became friendly with Sinatra's body guards and after the show they invited him to a party back at the Dorchester, where they were staying. As the entourage entered the hotel one of the Dorchester's security staff stopped the comic and asked who he was.

'That's Charlie,' Sinatra is reputed to have replied.

An act that I had come across while working in the north-east was hypnotist Tony Sands. I was there the night he hypnotised volunteers from the audience and got them doing all manner of silly things, including sucking a lemon thinking it was an orange. Tony had previously been a casino croupier and a singer before becoming a hypnotist. I booked him for a week at the El Piana and eagerly looked forward to a repeat of what I had witnessed up north.

There were only a handful of people in on the Sunday for his first night and Tony struggled in an attempt to hypnotise the four volunteers he had enticed on to the floor. They had been drinking and, after much giggling and play acting on their part, it was clear that the act wasn't working. At that point Tony called for the band to return to the stage and he finished his spot with some songs. The following Monday and Tuesday ended in similar fashion and Aubrey Gray was not happy about the fact that he had booked a hypnotist but was getting a singer instead.

Wednesday night off must have come as a great relief to Tony and on Thursday he arrived early armed with a strobe light. By now the word had got around about the hypnotist who couldn't hypnotise and that night the room was busy with people who had come to share in Tony's embarrassment. Just before he was due on Tony told me to be ready to turn off all the house lights when he asked.

There was a hush and Phoenix struck up a musical chord as I walked out on to the dance floor.

'Ladies and gentlemen, it's cabaret time.' I announced. 'Will you please put your hands together and welcome Tony Sands.' By now I had dropped the word hypnotist from my introduction.

Tony appeared. 'Good evening and welcome to the wonderful world of hypnosis.' I heard some people at a front table giggle.

He began as usual by asking the audience to put their hands together and imagine cement running through their fingers. The audience duly obliged and as the momentum in his voice quickened he gave me the nod to turn off the lights. I flicked the place into darkness and Tony switched on his strobe light.

'Listen to my voice and my voice only,' he demanded as atmospheric music played in the background. 'From now on I will be talking very loud and very fast and my voice is the only voice you will hear.'

The penetrating ray from the strobe cut through the darkness and created eerie shapes amongst the audience as Tony bellowed. 'Squeeze your hands together, tighter and tighter!'

There came the sound of a chair falling over and when Tony finally asked me to turn the lights back on I saw someone lying on the floor whilst others were sprawled across tables. Tony went to each individual and satisfied himself as to their condition before positioning them on chairs in a line on the cabaret floor.

Tony Sands now had his volunteers and he did a superb show. His subjects became transformed, went to the cinema and laughed at Laurel and Hardy and they became mischievous school children who pulled faces behind teacher Tony's back. Each was given a pair of glasses to try on whereupon they perceived the audience and themselves in the bargain, to be completely naked. One man even sucked a lemon, convinced it was an orange. The audience loved it and Tony's final two nights were sold out this time with people who did not come to mock.

Tony Sands didn't require his strobe light anymore and Aubrey Grey was a very happy man.

'What a great act,' he remarked.

There were three musicians in Phoenix; Steve Goodrum on drums, John Tubby the bass player and Pete McPhaull on keyboards. The fourth member Paul was the singer. When El Piana first opened I got up with the band and sang two or three numbers but gradually the amount of time I was spending on stage with them became longer.

Aubrey informed me one day that the club was not doing as well as he had hoped and that he would have to cut back on costs. By now I had become an integral part of the evening shows so Phoenix was offered the opportunity of continuing as a trio with me taking over the vocals.

Singer Paul didn't appear to be bothered either way and so the matter was quickly resolved.

18

Wednesday 13th December 1972 was originally set aside in my diary to watch a game of football. The circumstances however changed dramatically and the date became etched in my memory for a completely different reason.

Earlier that year, Lyn and I had moved from Hotblack Road into a bungalow in Pembrey Close when she became pregnant with our first child. Norwich City had reached the semi-finals of the League Cup – the first leg against Chelsea was being played at Stamford Bridge that Wednesday night and I had a ticket for the game. Just before I was due to leave home for London, Lyn went into labour. What had been anticipated as being a routine birth was suddenly fraught with complications and an ambulance was called.

Lyn had said that she wanted Ronnie Fisher to be present with her at the birth but, because of the problems, she was not allowed into the delivery room. Ronnie and I sat outside in the hospital waiting room as people rushed backwards and forwards. At one point I briefly saw someone carrying a small bundle, wrapped in a green blanket, quickly pass by. We waited there for ages, with no idea of what was happening, and it was past 8.00 p.m., more than nine hours since Lyn had first gone into labour, when I was asked if we had a name for our son.

In the weeks leading up to this day, Lyn and I had discussed various boys' names.

'Christian. Christian James' I replied instinctively.

It ended up becoming the most difficult breech birth and at one stage there seemed the possibility that our baby might not even survive.

* * *

I stayed on with Phoenix at the El Piana into the following year. By now the attendances at the club had fallen drastically and the weekly cabaret programme had been reduced to just one or two weekend nights. During the mid-week it was down to us in the band to carry the evening and keep what customers there were entertained. We were always pleased to see a hardcore gathering of regulars, which included Pauline Adams and her girlfriends. Pauline was the sister of Roger, an old school mate of mine and they, like most others, used the club as a late night drinking place after the pubs had closed. Consequently we usually spent the first two hours of an evening playing to virtually an empty house. Keith Skipper was also a regular. He was a journalist who worked for the local newspaper and eventually he went on to carve out a successful career for himself as both a radio presenter and an author. Keith was fond of soul music and one song in particular. I used to invite him to join us on stage where he would deliver his own rendition of Wilson Pickett's *In the Midnight Hour*.

* * *

In the late 1960's mobile discotheques had made their mark on the entertainment scene. Norwich Artistes had several DJ's on its books, including David Clayton and his Gemini Disco. David had contacted the office some time earlier seeking work and the agency provided him with bookings which, together with his own residency at the Canary public house, gave him the opportunity of resigning from his day job in a local music shop to promote Gemini Disco full time. As a professional DJ, David had little else to do with his time during the day and he took to hanging around our St Vedast Street office until eventually John Fisher suggested that he come in on a regular basis to answer the phones and make the tea. It was agreed that any disco bookings that came in would be offered first to David as recompense.

* * *

Geoff Fisher's changes in business continued when Ray Aldous took over the Melody Rooms. Ray already had two successful businesses in the city – the Gala Ballroom together with a bingo club on the outskirts. He was also remembered as the man who brought the Beatles to Norwich in 1963.

19

Ray Aldous completed the takeover of the Melody Rooms and announced his intention of turning it into a cabaret nightclub with John Fisher remaining in control of operations. Considerable refurbishment was to follow, beginning with a re-vamp of the existing stage and addition of a pull out platform extending into the audience for the cabaret acts to work on. Behind the wall that ran along the rear of the stage remained the original kitchen and up a flight of stairs to the right were three rooms, two of which were occupied. One was used as John's office and another served as a dressing room. The third was nothing more than a store room.

John Fisher thrived on the challenge of the new venture and he busied himself with drawing up plans for the alterations. He was now spending even less time in the office of Norwich Artistes and David Clayton came in more frequently to help me.

One day I received an unexpected visit from Ray Aldous. He'd come to tell me how the work was progressing at the Melody Rooms and emphasised how much more of John Fisher's time it would take up – not only would he be running the place at night, but during the day he would be dealing with general bookings and generating new business. Ray thought that it would be a good time, and opportunity, for David Clayton to take over John's partnership in Norwich Artistes. He made it sound like it was all his own idea but I got the distinct feeling that Ray had already discussed it with John before coming to see me. After he'd finally gone I talked everything over with David and a meeting with John Fisher was arranged.

When we arrived for the meeting Ray Aldous was also present. Although by now I was heavily involved with the majority of the agency business, John had always remained in total control of the finances. When the subject of money was raised, or questions regarding the debtors and creditors, John informed us that the only debts outstanding were domestic bills for running the St Vedast Street office.

Ray then made his presence felt by showing us the latest developments of the Melody Rooms. He spread the new plans out on a table and explained that the club was to be renamed the Talk of the East. The Talk of wherever it happened to be was quite a common name for a nightclub in those days – London had the Talk of the Town whilst Eccles in Manchester played host to the Talk of the North, Cornwall had Talk of the West, Carlisle, Talk of the Border and Southend, it's very own Talk of the South to name but a few.

Initially, Norwich's Talk was to operate for the public on Thursdays, Fridays and Saturdays with the remainder of the week available for private hire. As well as cabaret, there would also be dancing to a live band and disco. It was suggested that I come in as the compere, accompanied by Phoenix, whilst David was offered the position as the resident DJ.

David and I both warmed to the idea of the new venture. Ray offered Norwich Artistes the sole booking agency of all the entertainment for the venue and also said that we could have the use of the vacant room upstairs as our office, and what's more, we could have it rent-free. It had all sounded so very straight forward and cosy and an agreement was made.

We set about clearing the rubbish from the club's spare room and tidied its general appearance with a coat of paint. Our furniture was brought in from St Vedast Street and the phone lines switched over. In no time at all it was finished and we were in.

* * *

Not long after a tax bill, belonging to Norwich Artistes Limited, for just over two thousand pounds dropped through our letter box. We contacted John who insisted that this was now our responsibility. David and I were both angry that this unexpected liability had not been disclosed during our earlier meetings but John refused to budge and we were left with little option but to settle the outstanding sum. As scant consolation we still had the office rent free plus our evening work at a time when the bill from the Revenue proved a considerable drain on our resources.

In the early 1970's, opening a cabaret club almost anywhere else in the country would have been considered insane. For a number of years such venues which offered a glutton of live entertainment had been well supported by enthusiastic audiences but this form of entertainment was now on the wane. Even during the short space of time that I had been working the club circuits it was noticeable how once proud establishments were looking past their best due to a general lack of finance and public interest.

But here we were in Norfolk. It had always been said that the county was years behind the times.

Now was the time to prove that we were catching up and could buck the national trend.

20

On Thursday 11th April 1974, the Talk of the East, later to change its name to the Talk of East Anglia and eventually becoming known simply as the Talk, opened its doors to the public for the very first time. A fresh layer of tarmac had been applied to the car park and a neon sign displaying the name of the nightclub adorned the front. Those visiting the premises for the very first time might have been forgiven a certain amount of apprehension as they cast their eyes upon a building that had the unmistakable architectural appearance of something from the 1950's. Their fears however would soon be allayed when they stepped through the doors and were met with a transformation that was classic 1970's clubland.

Throughout the interior there had been new carpet fitted and the two long bars at either end of the main cabaret room had been renovated. There were raised seating areas to the front and either side of the dance floor that offered an excellent vantage point of the stage for over four hundred people. Directly opposite the stage was the booth that housed the DJ.

At 7.30 p.m. on that opening night, a queue of people made their way to tables that had been reserved in advance and, by the time Phoenix had begun their first live music set an hour later, the Talk of East Anglia was very busy and buzzing with excitement and anticipation.

I had booked two acts for the opening night. The Flirtations were a glamorous American vocal trio and Jerry Harris had appeared on *The Comedians* television show. A number of other comics from *The Comedians* would later prove popular attractions at the Talk but that night belonged to Jerry.

Another three-girl vocal act called Looking Glass appeared on the following two nights with comedy impressionist Roger Kitter topping the bill on the Saturday. The first three nights were an undisputed success and Jerry Harris had remarked just how good the venue was, and how warm and responsive the audience had been.

'I'll tell you what,' he said. 'This is a great room – comics will enjoy working here.'

* * *

I struck up an immediate friendship with Jerry and he invited me with Lyn and Christian to spend Christmas with him and his family at their home in Cheadle Hume in Cheshire. Our stay was most enjoyable, highlighted on Boxing Day, when we all went to a pantomime matinee in Manchester. No sooner had we made our way into the theatre than Jerry and I entered into the spirit of the occasion.

'It's behind you!' we informed the ice cream seller before the curtain had gone up and our repartee continued during the performance. I suddenly felt a tap on my shoulder and there stood the manager. He had been watching us for some time and told us that if we persisted in our antics he would have to ask us to leave.

'Cor,' said Jerry later. 'Can you believe it? Imagine if we'd been chucked out of a panto at our age!'

* * *

The amounts that the Talk paid its acts was sensibly based on the anticipated income generated from ticket sales and it was vital that this policy be maintained if the venue was to remain a success. The high amounts that some artistes were demanding, together with the recessionary times, were two contributing factors as to why a number of nightclubs throughout the country were shutting down. The general feeling was that, whilst the public would occasionally be prepared to pay more to see the bigger names, it was not a policy that could be adopted on a regular basis. The philosophy was to build a reputation for quality entertainment at a reasonable price so that people would know they were guaranteed a good night out regardless of who was appearing. To this end I once again turned my attention to the north of England and brought in three giants of clubland.

Benny Yorke came from Glasgow and had made TV guest appearances on the *David Nixon Show*, *Who Do You Do?* and the *Tommy Cooper Hour*. He was an offbeat and quite brilliant impressionist, best known for his numerous renditions of cartoon characters which rightly earned him the title of *The Man of a Thousand Voices*. Benny, in my opinion, was an entertainer who had never really achieved the full recognition that his talent so richly deserved when he passed away in 2002.

Lambert and Ross were an outstanding comedy double act featuring Peter Lambert as the straight man and his partner Willie Ross the comic.

Peter would be on stage, masquerading as an Italian opera singer, whilst Willie, in the guise as a member of the bar staff, busied himself around the tables. All eyes were on the stage and nobody took any notice of Willie who just so happened to be carrying a pile of trays. During a quieter moment of the act, Willie "accidently" dropped the trays causing a loud clatter. Peter then chastised Willie and dragged him up onto the stage where funny interactions took place. The end result was almost always a standing ovation. When the duo split in the eighties, Willie Ross went on to become a successful actor scoring film and television hits together with plays and stage appearances. He died at his Northampton home in 2000.

One of the truly great acts of those times was impressionist Dustin Gee. Dustin was the undisputed star of northern clubland and he personified the very highest quality level of both cool and camp. He was so very different and the manner in which he presented himself on stage was brilliant and diverse.

Whilst performing a routine based on TV's *University Challenge,* Dustin turned himself into a wickedly accurate caricature of a smug and smirking Bamber Gascoigne addressing both Queens College Oxford and Kings College Cambridge.

'And here's your starter for ten. Kings, I can offer it – Queens, can you take it?'

A quick turn, with his back to the audience, and suddenly he was a lipstick smeared and gravel-voiced Bette Davis, looking as if he'd just stepped straight out of *Whatever Happened To Baby Jane?*

Another transformation and he brought the house down as a facially perfect Robert Mitchum, waiting for the applause to die down before the quip 'I can't do the voice.' A change of mood and character and, with a hearty 'Hey-ho,' there he was as Larry Grayson.

After twenty years in show business, Dustin finally got his big television break on *Who Do You Do?* before forming a successful double act with Les Dennis.

Dustin and Les were the act that followed Tommy Cooper after he suffered a massive heart attack and died onstage during ITV's *Live from Her Majesty's* in April 1984. Dustin himself died from a heart attack just two years later.

I knew the talent that each of those three acts had to offer was beyond question and I was excited about showing Benny, Peter, Willie and Dustin off to the customers at the Talk. There is no substitute for excellence and there was never a doubt in my mind that the people of Norwich would take to them. One very pleasing factor was, despite them being virtually unknown in Norfolk, they had each succeeded in playing to well-attended audiences. The policy of offering a consistently high standard of entertainment for a reasonable outlay appeared to be working.

Hypnotist Tony Sands made a welcome return to Norwich, his first since the El Piana days. His appearance at the Talk attracted a large audience, including many who had never before seen a stage hypnotist. There were no shortage of volunteers when Tony called upon them to join him on stage and he returned to the venue time and time again becoming the venue's second biggest ever crowd-puller. The Talk of East Anglia's biggest attraction however happened almost by accident.

21

I received an invitation from Maurice King and Mary Arnold to attend the launch of a new band that Maurice was involved with. The band was called Blackwater Junction and it was clear that no expense had been spared when it was announced that the launch was taking place on a Sunday night at the London Palladium. Amongst the audience that night were a number of specially invited guests, including high-ranking agents and promoters. There was clearly a great expectation for Blackwater Junction to do well.

The two acts who appeared during the first half of the show were Benny Yorke and ventriloquist John Bouchier. When Blackwater Junction came on for the second half their volume was so loud that as many of the audience ended up outside in Argyll Street as remained in the theatre. Despite the array of talent on stage it wasn't Benny Yorke, John Bouchier or even Blackwater Junction who scored the success of the night.

'Ladies and gentlemen, will you please welcome your compere for the evening – Jimmy Jones!'

The audience erupted when Jimmy Jones strode out to the centre of the stage. He immediately launched into a barrage of quick-fire gags and a woman ran down the centre aisle to toss a bouquet of flowers at his feet. The response he received from the moment he was announced made it clear that this was someone who was known to the majority present. In their eyes he could do no wrong and at the end of the night I was told that a big risk had been taken by including Jimmy Jones on the bill. He was a very risqué comedian and had received strict instructions beforehand that he was not to deviate from anything but clean humour. I considered that if he could be that funny at the London Palladium, working under those restrictions, whatever would he be like if let loose on a crowd in a Norwich nightclub?

I called Jimmy's agent first thing next morning.

'Where is the venue?' asked Cyril.

'Norwich, in Norfolk,' I explained.

'Norwich.' said Cyril. 'It's a long way – he'll want at least ninety pounds.'

I told John Fisher about Jimmy Jones. John was taken back by the fee and said that ninety pounds was too much to pay for a support act.

'He's not a support act.' I replied. 'He's top of the bill,' and, after elaborating further on what I had witnessed at the Palladium, John was finally persuaded.

'Okay we'll give him a go,' he said.

The rest, as they say, is history. Jimmy Jones played the Talk of East Anglia on numerous occasions. During the late seventies he received an award from John Fisher and Ray Aldous, in recognition of putting more than ten thousand "bums on seats" at the venue, and he recorded a live album there to commemorate the achievement.

The Talk was considered a special place to be in the mid-seventies. There was not another venue like it for miles and it was always a great feeling to drive into Oak Street on a night and see a row of parked coaches that had brought audiences in from all over the county and beyond.

There was a genuine closeness and togetherness amongst the staff at The Talk and this was mainly down to John and Ronnie Fisher who regarded us all as one big happy family. Having painted such a rosy picture I have to point out that it wasn't always sweetness and light. Sometimes things didn't always go according to plan.

* * *

I booked the singer Lita Roza to appear. Lita had previously been a vocalist with the Ted Heath Band in the 1950's before becoming a television and recording star in her own right. A number of people, including local musicians who still held her in high esteem, had asked if we could get her and, despite initial reservations about her pulling power, she generated reasonable business and a healthy turn out for a Sunday night.

During her afternoon band-call with Phoenix, Lita had made little attempt to become on friendly terms with any of us. She maintained an air of aloofness as she ran through some of her numbers before announcing that she would next be singing a medley of her hits. Keyboard player Pete's music pad that she handed him was considerably bulky.

In the evening I introduced Lita. Her manner with the public remained similar to that with us during the afternoon. It seemed as if she was singing to herself and disregarding everyone else. She came to the part of her act when she announced the medley which seemed to breathe new life into the audience. Drummer Steve clicked in the tempo on his sticks and the music began.

Lita Roza launched herself into the medley with a new-found vigour. She pointed a finger to a man sitting at a front row table to announce that she was going to *Wash him Right out Of Her Hair* before suggesting to another that she might entice him into *Hernando's Hideaway*. With a whimper in her voice she sang of her *Secret Love,* lamenting that he had been locked up in *Allentown Jail.* There then followed a few bars of *I Could Have Danced All Night* before a further change of tempo. Now, totally in her stride, Lita was about to enquire as to the cost of *That Doggie in the Window* when suddenly there was silence from the keyboards.

Pete McPhaull had been frantically reading the music whilst flicking over the pages and because of his concentration he had failed to notice that the music pad was teetering on the edge of his keyboard. The folder had suddenly become top heavy and it concertinaed over the side of the instrument promptly followed by Pete. The drums and bass guitar spluttered to a halt.

Lita Roza stood alone in the middle of the cabaret floor and regained some of the composure she had temporarily lost due to the untimely and unexpected interruption. She turned and addressed the empty space behind the keyboard.

'Mister piano player,' she said. 'Can I have a B Flat?'

Pete poked his head up above the keyboard. His face was red and he was clearly very flustered.

'Oh plink bloody plonk!' he exclaimed, totally fed up with the whole situation. Lita Rosa stood expressionless. Plink bloody plonk were clearly notes that she did not recognise.

'Get her off,' hissed John Fisher.

In mid-turmoil, I was left with the unenviable task of bringing her performance to its premature end, whilst at the same time allowing her to exit with as much grace and dignity as possible.

Two other acts from Lita Roza's era that followed soon after thankfully enjoyed better success.

Comedian Tommy Trinder was a throwback to the days of music hall and variety. He was also the chairman of Fulham Football Club – his affiliation endorsed by the egg-stained club necktie that he wore. His catchphrase was "You lucky people," and the people who turned out to see him that night were indeed just that. During his act, Tommy announced that he had appeared in every theatre throughout the country.

'Played 'em all,' he proclaimed – and demonstrated just that by inviting members of the audience to shout out the names of different towns and cities. He then proceeded to reel off all the "Fun Palaces," as he called them, from those particular places.

Frankie Howerd was perhaps better known for his television and film roles than he was for being a stage comedian. He arrived for a Sunday night show with his pianist, a very elderly lady whom he referred to as Layby Lil. Frankie Howerd's comedic style was far removed from the much quicker and punchier delivery of Tommy Trinder. His stories were long and drawn out and accentuated with plenty of 'Oh yes madam' and 'Titter Ye Not.'

Although the audience in general took to him, there were one or two who weren't sure and felt that he had stolen bits of Jimmy Jones' act. I don't think so – Jimmy himself could not have been considered original and was perhaps more of a modern day Max Miller but without the subtlety.

Frankie Howerd made little effort to conceal his homosexuality and the Talk's very own David Clayton nearly got more than he had bargained for when he found himself alone with Frankie in the dressing room. David duly received an "approach" and, needless to say, declined the offer but he couldn't stop talking about it for weeks after.

22

'Norwich – it's a long way,' said Jim Bowen.

Since the opening night with Jerry Harris, other names from *The Comedians* had proven popular attractions at the Talk and I was keen to add Jim Bowen to the list. He lived in a converted railway station near the village of Carnforth in Lancashire and at first he was against the idea of the five-hour journey to Norwich. However, after a bit more persuasion, he finally agreed to come. Jim was just as funny off stage as he was on and he became an instant hit with the Norfolk public. The stories he told were embellished with so much colour and detail. He painted pictures in your mind and left the rest to the imagination.

Finding suitable accommodation for the acts that returned in the early hours of a morning and liked to sleep in late the next day presented a problem. The so-called pro-digs that were commonplace in clubland were not exactly in abundance in Norfolk. David Clayton's mother Rene however came to the rescue. She and her husband Reg were happy to provide a room. Rene was Yorkshire born and bred and her natural and warm northern charm shone through as she took to the role of landlady like a duck to water. Acts enjoyed their time with her and she treated them like her own. Jim Bowen stayed there and Rene would sometimes take him to task.

'Jim, you left this morning without having your breakfast.'

'Oh flippin' 'eck,' Jim would reply, suitably admonished.

Some of us would occasionally meet up for a liquid lunch at the Berni Inns restaurant in the city centre where manager Andy and his wife Rachel were excellent hosts. When he was in town Jim Bowen would join us and engage everyone with his stories. Fellow patrons having lunch at the restaurant would nudge one another on recognising Jim from the telly.

Jim Bowen and I had one major thing in common – we both supported Blackburn Rovers football team. Years later, during the heady days of the nineties when Blackburn was a force to be reckoned with, Jim invited me to a mid-week evening match at Ewood Park, Blackburn's home ground. I arranged to meet him there where we were to have dinner with the directors, watch the game and I was then to stay at his home overnight. I went by train up to Lancashire and was suited and booted for the occasion. With me I carried a case containing some casual clothes for travelling back the following day.

My taxi pulled up outside Ewood Park at 5.30 p.m. I had arrived earlier than expected and as I got out I could see a figure scurrying towards me.

'This way sir,' panted the figure and I duly followed. As we approached the entrance to the ground my escort informed me that my linesmen were already there. It seemed that my suited appearance and the case I was carrying, which he assumed contained my match kit, had convinced him that I was in fact the referee.

* * *

For a great number of entertainers, who made their living appearing in clubs, the motorways were the main arteries of travel to their places of work. There had been little reason for them to deviate from these well-trodden and familiar routes which stretched from north to south but now suddenly Norwich had found its way on to the map as the word spread about the new nightclub.

'Where's that?'

'The Talk of East Anglia.'

'Where's that?'

'Norwich – you know, in Norfolk.'

'Norfolk? That's a long way!'

By the time of the mid-seventies the fortunes of Norwich Artistes had improved considerably. Phil Beevis had taken a certain amount of business with him when he left and the agency was probably at its lowest ebb when David and I first took it over.

Despite the early unexpected financial setback we had to deal with, the Talk of East Anglia had proven beneficial to us long term and had without doubt helped raise our profile. Seeing the bigger names and the general quality of the acts that we were bringing into the county, there were new venues making contact and asking us to book their performers. The Talk also served as a social centre, allowing us an opportunity to catch up with some of our regular clients who went there for a night out.

* * *

We all had our own personal favourites from the acts who appeared at the nightclub. For John and Ronnie Fisher it was undoubtedly Fresh Aire.

Chris, Spike and Michael, who made up Fresh Aire, were an excellent vocal harmony outfit from Nottingham. Their big show-stopping number with which they closed their act was *The Holy City*. One day we were given the sad news that lead singer Michael had been diagnosed with Multiple Sclerosis. His condition deteriorated and his days on stage with Fresh Aire were numbered. It was fitting that his final appearance should take place at the Talk, whose audiences had embraced him time and time again. Michael was by now confined to a wheelchair and it was a tearful and emotional evening for everyone on a night which ended with three encores of *Jerusalem – The Holy City*.

Comedy is without doubt an acquired taste. Not everyone laughs at the same things, which certainly proved to be the case with an act that I never grew tired of watching.

Dave and Amos came from Swindon in Wiltshire. Their stage appearance was as dishevelled and bedraggled as their act, which defied logic and was best described as bordering on lunacy.

Dave carried a violin and Amos a mandolin. Amos displayed a fear of rats, with his phobia causing him to erupt into sudden moments of madness. They masqueraded as musicians but their intended masterpiece, bringing *The Merry Widow* to a climax before going straight into *The Student Prince,* never got off the ground as their act descended into more and more chaos. The performance was delivered in their delightful West Country accents and they were, without doubt, two of the funniest people I have ever had the pleasure of knowing.

Comic Lew Lewis appeared alongside them during a British Forces overseas tour. Landing back home at Brize Norton at the end of the tour they bid farewell to one another and Lew, who himself was not always the most rational of people, was heard to remark.

'And I hope I never see you two scatty bastards ever again!'

Lew Lewis came from that breed of comedian who believed that the world was out to steal their act. Call it insecurity or whatever but Lew was convinced that in every audience there were people with the sole intention of using his jokes for their own personal gain.

At this point I feel a certain amount of sympathy should be given to the comic who had the misfortune of following a girl singer on the same bill in a show. Some girl singers had a gag or two up their sleeve and, just before the comedian was due to go on, they would finish their spot with a joke which would inevitably be the same one that the comic had planned to open with.

Maxi Mann was a comedian who featured a knitting routine in his act. Coming across him one day I could not resist telling him.

'You'll never guess which singer is doing your knitting routine?'

He was livid. 'Never!' he exclaimed.

'Don't worry,' I replied. 'She's using different colour wool.'

* * *

There were two particular types of entertainment that went down well with the audiences at the Talk.

Recording stars from the sixties were always popular with the likes of Wayne Fontana and the Mindbenders, Freddie and the Dreamers, the Searchers, Joe Brown and the Bruvvers and the Merseybeats never failing to get the audience on their feet. One of the biggest crowd-pullers was Marty Wilde and the Wildcats. I booked Marty on many occasions, including the night when the show became well and truly a family affair. Fifteen year old daughter Kim joined ex-Vernon girl mum Joyce on stage as Marty's backing singers whilst son Ricky played keyboards with the Wildcats.

Drag acts, or *Cocks in Frocks* as they were sometimes referred to, were a big draw on the club circuit and we were fortunate in having one of the finest on our doorstep. Alan Kemp, better known to the public as Lana, lived in Suffolk and was a very glamorous Drag Queen. He told stories and sang live, unlike many of his contemporaries whose comedy routines were mimed to backing tapes. Lana was followed at the Talk by similar acts including the Dumbelles, Johnnie Peach and John and Ray, better known as the Mimetimers. Such was the popularity of Drag that we decided to put on a complete evening of it.

I booked Lana and the Mimetimers to headline the show and members of staff were encouraged to dress up accordingly. I sat with Phoenix and John Fisher in the dressing room whilst our make-up was applied and, after our wigs and frocks were finally added, we were ready to meet our public. Amid all our camping and revelry the door opened and in walked David Clayton dressed as a farmer.

We never worked out why David had decided on such an irrelevant costume theme that night. We eventually gave him the benefit of the doubt when it was suggested that he might still perhaps be suffering from *Post Frankie Howerd Traumatic Stress Disorder.*

23

Nobody could argue that the Talk didn't represent extremely good value for money. A night out, which included the admission, dinner and entertainment, cost as little as five pounds. The bar on the ticket price however was about to be raised when I found out that the American singing star Gene Pitney was to undertake a UK tour.

I knew the promoter responsible for bringing Pitney into the country and asked if there was any possibility of adding another date. I was told that Gene would be remaining in England for a few days after the tour had finished and another date, following his final show at the London Palladium, might be possible.

'Where is it?' I was asked.

'Norwich, in Norfolk' I replied.

'Norwich,' he said. 'That's not too bad.'

I went to John Fisher. Initially he was taken back by Gene Pitney's fee which was considerably more than he had ever paid for an act. He was however interested and set about doing some calculations.

The support act for Pitney's UK tour happened to be Jim Bowen. I spoke to Jim who said that he would be willing to compere the evening if our show went ahead. The Talk had been running a series of Sunday night talent competitions and it was considered a good idea to add the incentive of an appearance with Gene Pitney as part of the prize for the winning act.

The ticket price for the show had to be around twenty-five pounds per person to make it work. Would the people of Norfolk pay that much money? John made calls to some of his regular customers and was encouraged by the reaction. He said he would sleep on it and came back the following day with the decision that he wanted to go ahead.

The announcement of Gene Pitney received an immediate response. The admission charge included a three-course dinner and there was an early rush of calls from people who wanted to book tables.

I have often heard it said, never quite understanding the reasoning, that being in the entertainment business is not like having a proper job. Maybe people considered that the fun and enjoyment you can sometimes derive from it should be payment enough?

One of the Talk's regular customers was a garage proprietor who turned up most Saturdays quite late in the evening. He brought friends with him and, not bothered that there weren't any seats available, they were content to stand at the bar drinking. John usually let them in for nothing. This particular person called to enquire if he would be allowed in gratis for the Gene Pitney night. John explained about the high cost of the show and said that everyone would have to pay. The garage owner could not understand why he wouldn't be allowed in free of charge as normal as he would be spending money at the bar. With the conversation going nowhere, John finally suggested that he would allow him in if he could fill his car with free petrol at this person's garage.

'But that's my living,' came the reply.

I rest my case.

* * *

The date of the Gene Pitney show came around and every seat in the building had been sold. Extra tables had been squeezed into every nook and cranny to accommodate the overwhelming demand. The orchestra arrived mid-afternoon and Jim Bowen turned up soon after. Pitney's driver eventually pulled into the car park with his passenger. The atmosphere amongst the audience was electric and many of them had come armed with records and photos for Pitney to sign. We knew that it would have been difficult for him to make his getaway through the front entrance of the club after the show and I was given the task of taking him out through the rear of the building where it had been arranged for his driver to be waiting.

The evening began. Kirsten Price, the winning musical double act from our talent show, were given a warm reception by the audience and Jim Bowen soon had them laughing. Then came the moment everybody had been waiting for.

The lights darkened as the members of the orchestra took up their positions on the stage. Musical Director Maurice Merry was seated at the piano – he raised an arm and, with the wave of an imaginary baton, he sparked off the unmistakeable strains of *Twenty-Four Hours from Tulsa* which led into an overture of recognisable Pitney songs. Then came a momentary silence before the orchestra struck up again. The stage suddenly became flooded in light and there was the person they had all come to see. The place erupted and for the next seventy-five minutes the hits were delivered, one after another. Maurice Merry handed Pitney pieces of paper, collected from members of the audience, which contained messages and requests. Then, all too soon it seemed, came the final number.

'Ladies and gentlemen, once again for Gene Pitney,' yelled Jim Bowen, trying to make himself heard above the screams and shouts for more. It seemed that some of the audience had already anticipated a quick exit by the star and had left their seats to head for the foyer but as Gene Pitney came off stage I was waiting. I led him through the kitchen, beyond the bottle store and out through the rear exit crash doors only to arrive at a dismally bleak and empty Chatham Street. The car was not there.

'It will be here in a minute,' I assured Gene and we waited. Ten minutes passed by and there was still no sign of the car. By now it had started to rain so we went back inside the bottle store until we heard the sound of an engine and at last the vehicle arrived.

The foyer had been crowded with the overspill of people waiting for Gene Pitney to leave and during the mayhem Pitney's car had been blocked in by a taxi. Some of the women were crying – their mascara-stained faces showing anguish and despair on the realisation that their time with their idol was over.

Little did they realise that only a short distance away, hidden behind a few bricks and plasterboard, sat the man himself.

24

At Norwich Artistes, David and I undertook different roles. He looked after the bookings for the bands and discos whilst I handled the cabaret and variety side of the business. There had also been an increase in the number of requests for local celebrities to attend fete openings and the like. With this additional demand we established representation of some Norwich City footballers together with regional BBC and Anglia TV presenters. David had also become involved with broadcasting for local hospital radio.

We were paid a visit by Chic Applin. Chic was the band leader from the Norwood Rooms in Norwich and was also responsible for booking the summer entertainment into a number of holiday parks dotted along the Norfolk and Suffolk coastline. Chic's agency business was predominantly seasonal and he told us that he had been taking a keen interest in the way that we had reshaped and developed Norwich Artistes. He thought it possible that our two offices could work together which would prove beneficial to both, offering him more of an all-year round trade whilst in turn giving us a foot in the door of the summer season business. Chic also mentioned that he was looking for a band for a six nights per week summer season at a holiday centre near Great Yarmouth.

During the summer attendances at the Talk dropped and we considered it a good idea that I take the season with Phoenix and another band be brought in to replace us at the Talk during the months we would be away.

* * *

The first time I saw Karen Kay on stage was at the Wellington Theatre in Great Yarmouth. Karen was a singer, comedienne and impressionist all rolled into one and she simply oozed class. Her vocal range was phenomenal – one minute she was Barbra Streisand singing *Don't Rain on My Parade* and the next, an impression of "Killer" (Cilla) Black with a parody of *The Liverpool Lullaby* delivered in a very thick and exaggerated Scouse accent.

'*Oh you are a mucky kid – dirty arse* (pause for laughter) *a dustbin lid. When he finds out what you did – you'll gerra belt from your daad…*'

I booked Karen to appear alongside Warren Mitchell at the Talk. She told me of a charity that she was involved with called Stars Organisation for Spastics and she suggested that the Talk might be a good venue to stage one of their shows.

One day she brought her seven-year old son into our office to meet us.

'This is Jason,' she said. 'Jason say hello to Brian and David.'

Jason shyly mumbled his hellos.

'One day he wants to be a singer, don't you Jason.' Karen told us and Jason nodded.

After meeting that shy and skinny little boy that day, neither of us ever imagined that Jason would eventually grow up to become Jay Kay of the British funk band Jamiroquai.

I followed Karen Kay's career with interest – through her halcyon days of headlining in theatres and starring in her own television show, up until the time in the eighties when she, like so many others, suffered as television fell out of love with variety.

When her theatre work dried up, I booked Karen for a summer season in holiday parks and then into working men's clubs during the winter months. The orchestras that once played for her were now reduced to a venue's resident organist and drummer. It was sad to see her decline and a letter I received from her soon after another run of social club bookings said all there was to be said about the state of the business at that time.

'Dear Brian, please find enclosed the commission for a week of fuck-ups somewhere in Wales.'

***

Warren Mitchell's appearance with Karen Kay at the Talk did excellent business. Warren was an acclaimed English actor who rose to initial prominence in the role of bigoted cockney Alf Garnett in the television sitcom *Till Death Us Do Part*. He had successfully transferred the character to the stage and the actor's preparation for his performance was meticulous. Warren naturally looked like Alf Garnett but it was only when a moustache was applied that the transformation became complete.

'Alf, you're back,' he remarked to himself in the mirror and from that moment on he remained in character until the time he left the stage.

Warren Mitchell displayed a sense of loyalty to the people who looked after his interests.

When we brought the bigger household names to the area we sometimes arranged interviews for them with the local media. Such an interview was planned with Warren for the BBC and I drove both him and David to the Corporation's studio in Norwich. On the way we passed by the Samson and Hercules ballroom which Warren recognised as a place where he had spent some of his time whilst stationed at Bircham Newton with Richard Burton during the war. When we arrived at the BBC we were told that the studio was not big enough to accommodate us all and David and I would have to wait outside. Warren would have none of it.

'These are my friends,' he said. 'If they are not allowed in then neither am I.'

Warren got his way. He did the interview whilst David and I were allowed to watch from the Gallery.

25

Chic Applin received a call from Albert Stevenson. The two of them went back a long time, to the days when Albert had been the booker of entertainment for the Pontins Organisation and Chic had provided acts for some of its east coast venues. Albert was now the Producer for ATV's *New Faces* and he asked if Chic would be interested in putting on a showcase of acts he might consider for the programme. A date was arranged for the auditions to take place at the Talk. We had originally intended making this a strictly invitation only affair but the word soon got out and a number of other acts asked if they could be included.

On the day it became painfully obvious that some of the candidates we had selected to attend should not have been considered for the auditions. They included some very blue comedians and, as one launched into a story about a nun and a garden vegetable, Albert cut him short.

'Now listen to me everyone,' he said addressing the remaining acts. He reminded them that they were auditioning for a national family television show and if anybody else intended telling jokes like the one he had just been subjected to they were not to bother. Albert was clearly not happy.

Next up was a well turned out woman who positioned herself at her keyboard whilst the comedians still waiting to be seen retreated to far-flung corners of the building in order to rethink their acts. The lady at the keyboard had a pleasant singing voice and Albert Stevenson smiled his approval. She finished her song and proceeded to tell a joke about a woman's sanitary item.

From the number of acts that had auditioned during that long and very tiring day, Albert booked six for the programme. Two other local acts, Peter Collins with Style and Chris North and Jill, were known to Albert from his Pontins days and independently they both found themselves on the show. With the consideration that we might be asked to put on further auditions in the future, Chic, David and I decided to form a management company.

* * *

New Faces was recorded on a Wednesday night from Central TV's Broad Street studios in Birmingham and we travelled to the West Midlands whenever our acts appeared. The programme's judging panels varied from agents and managers to radio DJ's, variety artistes and record producers. All of our acts gave good accounts of themselves as did Peter Collins with his band Style and illusionists Chris North and Jill.

Chris North and his wife Jill were a well presented and polished magic double act with Jill looking every part the magician's glamorous assistant. To her advantage, she had all the attributes that a magician's glamorous assistant should have. It was once said that Chris could produce a ten ton elephant from his trouser pocket and the audience would still be staring at Jill's cleavage.

Peter Collins with Style won their particular heat by performing a Matt Monro number called *Sarah's Coming Home* which received high praise from the judging panel.

'That's a lovely song,' remarked Albert afterwards. 'Do that in the final and you've a chance.'

There was certainly optimism that the band might be successful. One of the national tabloids ran a feature on each of the finalists, together with their ratings of success, and Peter Collins with Style was up there amongst the favourites.

Peter however chose not to heed Albert Stevenson's advice and instead he decided on performing the Richard Harris number *MacArthur Park*. The song lacked the sentiment and appeal of *Sarah's Coming Home* and, with its over-busy arrangement, it became not so much a performance, but more a musical battle between the three musicians of Style and the programme's Musical Director Johnny Patrick who was leading his orchestra in a different studio. The gamble with the number failed and Peter Collins sank down the leader board.

One person who did go on to make a name for himself following an audition in Norwich was Joe Pasquale but the most successful act we looked after who emerged from *New Faces* was a magician and mind reader.

* * *

Graham P Jolley's deadpan humour, together with his dexterity in manipulation and uncanny ability to seemingly read people's minds, was second to none. His style of presentation was unique.

I had started to book Graham the year before and, as his reputation and subsequent popularity grew, I ended up acting more as his manager. I promoted him with total belief in what he had to offer and succeeded in, not only increasing the number of his bookings, but also his fees. By the time his *New Faces* final came around, Graham's status in the business had soared considerably. He was now in demand for high profile events and added a cruise ship appearance onboard Cunard's prestigious QE2 liner to his name.

On the *New Faces* final Graham produced yet another outstanding performance which had bookers raving and not long after that his first appearance on the famous Las Vegas strip followed. In America Graham worked alongside some of the finest magicians in the world and he returned home armed with new tricks which he employed with spectacular effect.

I booked Graham to appear at London's Palace Theatre on a Sunday night variety show. We arrived at the theatre during the afternoon to discover that Graham was sharing a dressing room with the celebrated actor Ron Moody who was also on the bill, reprising his brilliant portrayal of Fagin from the musical *Oliver*. The rehearsals were in full flow and as we waited for our call, Ron sat quietly studying a crossword whilst puffing on his pipe. Suddenly an announcement came through the dressing room speakers.

'Mr Moody, on stage if you would please.'

Ron Moody downed his pen and pipe and suddenly there he was, in total character and once more, *Reviewing the Situation*.

26

Back in Norwich, the Talk continued to be the region's number one cabaret venue and with its reputation came the never-ending challenge of finding new names to fill the programme. Jimmy Jones and Tony Sands always ensured full houses whenever they appeared and there were a few other acts who had also established their own followings. The Ivy League proved popular and Fresh Aire, now featuring new member Tony Harding, continued to generate their own demand. Marty Wilde was also guaranteed to sell out but these names were not enough.

It was a proven fact that the acts with television exposure were more likely to sell out with the public.

The Barry Lee Show underwent dramatic changes following the departure of lead singer Barry. The remaining members, with drummer Angus Jarvis becoming their Musical Director and keyboard player Tony Young newly recruited, reinvented themselves as the Brother Lees and came up with the idea of a triple-impressions act that turned around their fortunes. Their name alone had always ensured a reasonable turn-out but it was not until Roger, Michael and Tony had made appearances on Bruce Forsyth's *The Generation Game* that their popularity increased considerably and they became an established national clubland attraction.

New Faces produced its fair share of acts, including Jim Davidson, Les Dennis and Lenny Henry whose careers have all achieved longevity. It was not long after he had won the show that Lenny Henry came to Norwich and his stage act was basically the collective material that he had performed on television together with other bits of business added to make up the time. Lenny of course eventually went on to establish himself both as a successful comedian and actor and was always up for a laugh.

On one occasion, when I had him booked in Bournemouth, he engaged in horse play with my son Christian who was chasing him and trying to spray him with shaving cream in an attempt to turn him white.

Jim Davidson was a very confident individual when I first booked him for a tough military audience. Although he was still relatively young, Jim proved himself to be a fearless comedian and, even when confronted by the most critical and heavyweight of crowds, he was able to come back at them with his arsenal of hard-hitting adult humour.

Even more so than *New Faces, The Comedians* became the conveyor belt that produced many household names in the seventies. I have already mentioned Jerry Harris and Jim Bowen and I can also add Mike Reid, Jimmy Marshall, Stan Boardman, Mike Burton, Colin Crompton, Duggie Brown, George Roper, Charlie Williams, Ken Goodwin and Roy Walker to the list of comics from Granada's Manchester studios that came to Norwich.

* * *

One man from *The Comedians* I have deliberately reserved for a special mention is Bernard Manning. Bernard courted controversy wherever he appeared with an act that was considered racist, sexist and highly offensive. His audiences were predominately male and consisted of hecklers who delighted in hurling insults at the stage knowing that Bernard would always come back at them, giving twice as good as he got. Despite his public image, Bernard Manning was as pleasant and genial a person as you could ever wish to meet.

Because of his reputation, Bernard's television appearances after *The Comedians* had been limited. One TV show however on which he did feature was the popular children's programme *Tiswas*. The show was hosted by a young Chris Tarrant and broadcast live on a Saturday morning. Any live broadcast was considered to be pressure enough and Bernard on the show only added to the anxiety amongst the production team.

Also appearing one morning was Lenny Henry. During the first part of the programme Bernard and Lenny performed a sketch based on *Roots,* the TV drama about the African slave-trade. In the sketch Bernard played a white hunter and was kitted out in khaki shorts and pith helmet whilst Lenny was cast as a black slave.

'Come here Kunta Kinte,' demanded Bernard beckoning to Lenny.

'I think I said that right,' adlibbed Bernard and Lenny stifled a snigger.

Later in the programme there was an appearance from Shirley Crabtree, better known as the wrestler Big Daddy. He was followed by Tony Brutus, a strong man act from Liverpool. Tony produced a neck and shoulder harness which was about six feet in length and had a chair suspended by a chain at either end. He invited Big Daddy, who weighed in at twenty-seven stone, to sit in one of the chairs and Bernard Manning, no beanpole himself, to sit in the other. Tony Brutus then addressed everyone in the studio, asking them to agree that the collective weight of the two volunteers he intended lifting was considerable. They agreed unanimously.

Big Daddy and Bernard wedged themselves into their chairs, their feet touching the ground. Tony Brutus then took the weight and prepared to lift his cargo. He groaned, he grunted, he strained, and someone said he even broke wind, as he summoned every ounce of strength in his body in his effort to succeed. And succeed he did, but only just.

Both Shirley Crabtree and Bernard Manning were momentarily airborne when Tony's legs buckled and gave way. The entire spectacle clanged, clattered and crashed its way to earth reducing both the exponent and participants into heaps of rolling mass. As a result of his endeavour Tony Brutus damaged his leg and didn't work again for six months. To add insult to injury, after getting off the floor and dusting himself down, Bernard announced.

'You know what Tony. Your act is worth more as scrap!'

27

My train pulled into Colchester station and I was met by a driver who took me to the nearby Prested Hall Centre. I had travelled to Essex to explore further the possibility that Karen Kay had previously mentioned to me about staging a charity show in Norwich.

The Stars Organisation for Spastics was a charity formed in 1953 by Dame Vera Lynn for sufferers of cerebral palsy. When I arrived at the Prested Hall Centre I was introduced to the foundation's committee members, who included the entertainer Dickie Henderson. SOS, as it is recognised, was interested in knowing more about the Talk of East Anglia.

John Fisher had already said that he would be willing to stage such an event and, after a great deal of discussion that day, it was agreed that SOS would present a show in Norwich. A Sunday was considered to be the best night to do it and a date was duly set. Dickie Henderson announced that he himself would appear and said that he would advise me later of the other acts who would also be taking part.

Within a few days the veteran comedian Arthur Askey had been confirmed on the bill along with Karen Kay. *New Faces* presenter Derek Hobson was to compere the evening and the musical backing would be in the hands of pianist Pat Dodd and his musicians. Danny La Rue, who was headlining in his own summer show in nearby Great Yarmouth at the time, also agreed to make a guest appearance and present the raffle. After further deliberation, and in order to create more local interest, I received confirmation that I could include Peter

Collins with Style together with local beauty queen Janice Lea who held the title of *Miss Talk of East Anglia* and more recently, TV's *Miss Anglia,* to the line-up.

The public lent their support and a sell-out evening was ensured. At the far end of the club there was a small back room with a bar and this became the VIP lounge. In there a reception and buffet was prepared for the artistes and guests.

* * *

Arthur Askey arrived late afternoon. He had informed me that he would be bringing his sister and had requested that two rooms be reserved for them at a local hotel. In consideration of his advanced years, he had been scheduled to open the show in case he decided that he wanted to leave early.

And open the show he most certainly did. Arthur burst onto the stage and delivered a performance of boundless energy. The way he could manipulate a crowd with his use of audience participation was masterly and the people responded to his every whim. After rightly receiving a standing ovation he returned to the VIP lounge whereupon he resumed his assault on the buffet.

The rest of the evening ran smoothly. Karen Kay produced her usual faultless performance of singing and impressions whilst Dickie Henderson demonstrated why he was consider-ed the master of his craft, best highlighted by his excellent clowning during his bar stool routine. Peter Collins wowed the ladies and Derek Hobson held it all together nicely whilst Janice Lea proved to be the perfect assistant for Danny La Rue during the raffle.

The evening had been a success and it was satisfying to know that all the time and effort in putting it together had been worthwhile. Despite the consideration that had been shown for his age, Arthur Askey's stamina knew no bounds. He was one of the last to leave that night and the following morning Arthur and his sister departed their hotel without paying the bill.

It was left for me to settle the account.

* * *

Private functions were a vital financial cog in preserving the fortunes of the Talk. Two annual events in particular stand out in my memory.

The East Anglia division of the Police Federation of England and Wales event was attended by the hierarchy of the force together with a guest list that included a number of the prominent local gentry. Security for this event was always of the highest level, no more so than when the bomb threats and attacks by the IRA were at their most fierce. On those occasions sniffer dogs were brought into the building beforehand to ensure that every possible place where a device could be concealed was checked out.

At one Police Federation event I arrived to find an area of the car park roped off and inside the cordon was a highly polished black limousine displaying a crest on the bonnet. I was informed that Princess Anne herself was attending the event that night as the guest of honour.

The speeches and awards ceremony had already taken place by the time I'd arrived and I assumed that Princess Anne had been there to make the presentations.

When it came to the music spot by Phoenix, the crowd on the dance floor had swelled considerably obstructing what sighting I might have had of our royal visitor. I considered the evening to be our very own Royal Command Performance and instinctively I found myself bowing discreetly each time I turned in the direction where I anticipated she might be sitting. At the end of the night, with still no sighting of our special guest and an aching back, I was informed by our resident team of doormen pranksters that the shiny black limousine had not belonged to Princess Anne after all and was in fact the charge of some local council dignitary.

The Talk also played host to an annual hare-coursing event that was the most lavish of affairs. The function was always well attended and the guests included land owners and members of the farming fraternity – some of them symbolising their sport by wearing a silver hare on a chain around their necks. There are probably a great number of people who regard hare coursing, like fox hunting, as barbaric. The Hunting Act of 2004 officially outlawed it as an illegal blood sport banned nationally although before then it was still common practice in Norfolk.

The evening began as usual with a dinner followed by the presentations in recognition of various achievements in the field of hare coursing. After the presentations came the draw for the raffle. Raffle prizes usually consisted of bottles of wine, boxes of chocolates and the like but the hare coursing raffle was no ordinary raffle. The hare coursing raffle was in a league of its own. The holders of the winning tickets would step up to receive their Waterford crystals, pop-up toasters and television sets.

Presiding over the proceedings was the President, who was seated at the top table flanked by two nuns. The nuns were from the order of *The Little Sisters of the Assumption,* their convent situated nearby. Adorned in their black and white habits, they sat quietly throughout the dinner and formalities until it was time for them to be introduced to the guests. The nuns made this annual pilgrimage to receive a cheque donated to their order on behalf of the hare coursing club.

The President rose to his feet.

'Ladies and gentlemen,' he announced in his broad Norfolk accent. The considerable sum of money raised was then disclosed to the audience and followed by the introduction of the two guests of honour.

The President introduced them as, 'the little sisters of the 'sumption,' and, to encourage a louder and more enthusiastic response, he beseeched a big 'Come on, let's hear it for the little sisters.' The nuns duly stood up to rapturous applause and humbly accepted the cheque before taking their leave.

I have never understood the connection between hare-coursing and a convent of nuns. Maybe it was considered that the money donated might buy penance and offer a greater opportunity of absolution in the afterlife.

***

The Silver Jubilee of Elizabeth II marked the twenty-fifth anniversary of Queen Elizabeth II's ascension to the thrones of the United Kingdom and other Commonwealth realms. It was celebrated in 1977 with street parties and parades throughout the country. The royal household of the Queen's Sandringham Estate were organising their own Silver Jubilee celebration and contacted Norwich Artistes asking if we could provide a dance band. It was requested that the band should play some traditional highland jigs and reels as there were guests from Scotland who would be attending.

After the event had taken place I made my follow-up call and spoke with the organiser who confirmed that the evening had been a considerable success and that the band had been well received. I asked how the Scottish music had been received.

It happened that the band had only played a small selection of the traditional songs due to the fact that some of the guests were quite incapacitated after overindulging in the celebrations. Flinging themselves about with jigs and reels had been the last things on their minds that night.

28

Despite his traumatic birth, Christian made a bright start to his school days and he thrived, especially in athletics, where he sometimes found himself competing against, and beating, boys much older than himself.

Occasionally I would take him with me to the Talk where it was not uncommon for him to find himself in the company of people he recognised from the world of television. When he began to talk about these people at school his teachers considered that his imagination was running away with him; it was only after the situation had been explained that the school realised Christian's fantasy world was in fact a reality.

As a family we managed to get ourselves away for holidays abroad. We went to Malta, which I was familiar with having booked acts into the Preluna nightclub in Sliema.

Malta had a reputation as being a peaceful country but its peace and tranquillity was interrupted on the day we hired a car and boarded a ferry to visit the nearby island of Gozo. During the crossing a thin dark pencil line appeared on the horizon which gradually got bigger so that by the time we disembarked it had become quite substantial. As I drove the car off the ferry there was a loud crack of thunder and the ground beneath us shook. Torrential rain followed and by the time we reached the town of Victoria the surface water had risen and was ankle deep. It was only later, when we finally arrived back in Malta, that we discovered we had been on the receiving end of an earthquake that had originated in Sicily.

Our holiday to Tunisia certainly had its moments too. At that time our daughter Natalie was no more than a toddler.

One day during the holiday we decided to take a coach trip from our hotel and visit Tunis the capital, some fifty miles from where we were staying. Along the way our coach was in collision with a small girl who had been playing by the roadside. There was a great deal of commotion as the child appeared to be badly injured. Someone suggested that we should take her to a hospital but our driver explained that it was pointless as she would not receive any treatment without prior payment. A collection was then swiftly arranged by the coach party. By this time the child's mother had appeared on the scene and she boarded the coach cradling the motionless child in her arms.

We arrived at the hospital, a dismal place and in a bad state of repair. Outside there were blankets and stained mattresses on which the sick, without money and very little chance of being cared for, were lying. We left the mother and her daughter at the hospital and made our way on to Tunis. Later we heard rumours that the child had been abandoned outside the hospital. It was likely the easier and more expedient option of the mother to have another baby and pocket the money that she had received from our collection.

When we finally arrived in Tunis we visited a bazaar which was basically a local market. It was situated within high wall-ed quarters comprising alleyways of shaded and narrow streets that were crammed with vendors selling all manner of goods. We pushed Natalie in her buggy whilst Christian followed idly behind. After a while we became aware that Christian was no longer with us. We were immediately overcome with panic and I ran back to where we had been walking. I barged my way through the out-stretched arms of traders and beggars when suddenly I heard a cry and there was Christian standing with a man and a woman.

He had managed to get himself separated from us and had become lost and alone when the man and woman came across him. Thankfully they were staying at the same hotel as us and had recognised Christian. They had hired a car to visit Tunis that day and it was pure chance that they had decided to visit the same bazaar as us.

During our stay some local traders arrived on the beach outside our hotel. They brought camels and, parading them, they encouraged us tourists to take part in camel racing. I did not take a lot of encouraging and was placed in the third and final race. My turn came and at the starting post the six camels bunched themselves together with their handlers standing behind them, tugging at their tails and trying to organise the creatures into some semblance of a line. A group of onlookers from the hotel had gathered further down the beach and were waiting in anticipation at the winning post. Despite all the efforts of the handlers the camels continued to shuffle around in different directions when abruptly a flag was waved and the race began.

My knowledge of camels is practically non-existent. I have no idea of their life span or how long they can survive in the desert without water. What I did learn that day however is that, when a sharp object is applied with a forceful stab to its genitals, the camel's immediate response is to run in whatever direction in which it is facing at the time.

My camel headed out towards the open sea – whether it was to escape a further assault on its testicles, or hoping that the cold water might ease the throbbing between its legs, we shall never know. The handler frantically clung to its tail but the camel continued to wade out even further into the sea. As the water rose to my knees I pulled hard at the reins in an attempt to persuade it to stop. This totally failed to halt its progress – I had pulled its head back so far that I was practically gazing down its nostrils with the creature snorting and spitting aggressively. To those viewing the spectacle from afar, the camel, now almost fully submerged apart from its neck might well have resembled the Loch Ness Monster towing a water skier with me a helpless figure stranded atop.

At last the camel decided that enough was enough and it gave up the fight allowing its distressed handler to reverse it out of the Mediterranean and back up the beach. I released my grip on the reins and breathed a sigh of relief.

When I finally arrived back at the hotel the crowd had dispersed. The winners of the first two camel races were celebrating at the bar. I had nothing to celebrate and received no more than a 'huh!' from Lyn when I caught up with her later. She, like the others, had given up on me at the beach.

29

Norwich Artistes got involved in providing people as extras for television work.

In the seventies, the cast of *Monty Python* arrived in Norfolk to film a new series. To any ardent *Python* fans, the Alan Whicker and Whicker Island sketch in particular will stand out in the memory. The filming took place at Winterton-on-Sea near Great Yarmouth and in one scene John Cleese was sat naked at a piano facing the sea with his back to the camera. We had booked a young lady to also appear in that scene. I will not embarrass her by mentioning her name but her task was very simple – she had to run across the background completely nude.

Years later we began to receive cheques from the BBC. The cheques were made out to the young lady in question. They were her royalty payments for repeats of the programme in far-reaching parts of the world. We had no idea where she might now be living and so we launched an appeal for her to come forward and claim her just rewards. She never did and I suspect that a once happy-go-lucky free spirit had long since matured into a grown-up and sensible woman with no desire to be being re-associated with her past.

* * *

Anglia Television was filming a sitcom called *Backs to the Land*, a story about land army girls during the Second World War. Not long after filming had begun I received a visit from Teri Stevens who was a member of the cast. She told me that as well as being an actress she was also a singer and a dancer so during her stay in Norfolk I came up with some bookings for her. When the filming was over and it was time for her to leave Teri thanked me for my efforts and told me that she was off to seek her fame and fortune. Sometime later she sent me a photograph of herself, taken alongside the legendary Lucille Ball, backstage in Las Vegas where Teri had been appearing with Sammy Davis Junior.

* * *

The BBC made a drama called *Woman in White* with the actors Diana Quick, Ian Richardson and Jenny Seagrove cast in the starring roles. Part of the filming was to take place in Norfolk and the Corporation had requested we find a young boy to play the part of a street urchin. I saw this as an opportunity of justifying Christian's earlier suspected wayward imagination and contacted his school telling them of the type of character the BBC was seeking. Here was an opportunity not only to approach Christian's school with a view to recruiting a suitable character from their pool of pupils, but in doing so to demonstrate once and for all to the teachers there that my son's frequent references to his intimate knowledge of the entertainment industry were indeed not the symptoms of a wayward imagination. The school notified the parents of some pupils and eventually I had seven candidates who might fit the bill. I sent their details off to London and added Christian's as the eighth.

The casting team from the production company then came to Norwich to interview the children. Each one was auditioned and eventually it was Christian who was selected for the role. Parents of the other children might be forgiven for suspecting that favouritism had played a part in the final decision but that most certainly was not the case. At nine years old, and with his longish hair, freckles and cheeky grin, Christian looked every bit a street urchin.

* * *

Thanks to the number of productions being filmed around East Anglia extra work provided an additional income for the entertainers who earned their living from performing. It was also an opportunity for those who had never stepped onto a stage in their lives but had somehow managed to obtain membership to the actors' union Equity. They mixed with the professionals acting out the dramas.

My own personal experiences of appearing as an extra were born out of need to make up the numbers more than anything else.

In 1985 the BBC made a documentary called *Soldiers: A History of Men in Battle*. It told the story of the history of warfare from antiquity to the Falklands war. Conflicts of the twentieth century were shown using genuine film footage but for earlier ones extras were engaged to re-enact the battles.

I became a soldier of a heavily defeated army retreating from battle sometime during the nineteenth century. Because there were so many extras involved the BBC had to hire additional costumes and, in order to look war worn, those of us wearing the Corporation's own uniforms were told to roll down a hill into puddles of mud and water whilst those in the hired costumes that had to be returned in good condition made do with a more restrained smearing of muck and dirt.

In one particular scene I was one of the badly injured and dying who were laid out inside a makeshift hospital. Some of us appearing in close-ups were made up – I had an ugly gaping and bloody bayonet wound glued to my forearm. A track, on which the camera shooting the carnage was situated, wound its way around our bodies.

The director appeared blasting out instructions through his megaphone.

'Okay,' he said. 'Everyone quiet please and when I shout action I want lots of moaning and groaning.' The camera began its journey towards us.

Lying beside me was the comedy duo Deakin and Dean and moaning and groaning were duly delivered.

'Oh my piles' wailed Dean, alias comedian Maxi Mann. This induced sniggers from the dying followed by a cry of 'Cut' from the director.

'Okay let's go again' he instructed, clearly a patient man. 'And remember, quiet until I shout action.'

The camera once again whirred into motion along the track as the silence was broken by the rasping sound of an almighty fart causing eruptions of uncontrollable laughter throughout the infirmary.

'Cut!' screamed the director.

My only other experience as an extra came during the popular series of *Lovejoy* which starred Ian McShane as the endearing roguish antique dealer. I provided a number of people for a scene involving a cricket match set in a picturesque Suffolk village and when we all turned up, dressed in whites as requested; I discovered that Bob Hannam and me were the only two who had ever played the game. Consequently we were given the ball to bowl until one of us managed a delivery close enough for the batsman at the other end to hit it.

And that was me done with the film business. I enjoyed the camaraderie on set but not the endless hours spent sitting around waiting to be called. My biggest disappointment was during *Lovejoy* when I overslept for an early morning shoot in a supermarket where, during a fight scene, I was to have been pushed through a towering display of tinned baked beans.

30

John Fisher came up with the idea of forming a Gentleman's Sporting Club and announced a series of boxing and snooker black tie dinners. The first snooker event featured the controversial Alex Higgins.

Alex had a widely reported drink problem which sometimes resulted in an unpredictable manner. Unbeknown to us, he had been booked somewhere else in the afternoon prior to his evening exhibition match at the Talk. When he finally arrived it was quite apparent that he had been drinking and we rightly suspected that we might be in for an unpredictable evening.

He had gained the title of Hurricane Higgins due to the power with which he dispatched snooker balls but that night, such was the ferocity of his shots, the balls were not only missing the pockets but some actually ended up in the laps of spectators seated in the front rows. His behaviour was disgraceful and a big let-down for the members who had paid good money to see him.

Fortunately a while later, Jimmy White came and restored some credibility to both the sport and to the Gentleman's Sporting Club.

Steve Davis was the world's number one snooker player at the time when he found himself filming in Norwich on the same night that Bernard Manning was appearing at the Talk. Steve happened to be a big fan of Bernard's and phoned to ask if he could come and see the show after he'd finished at the studio.

Later that night Steve Davis met Bernard backstage and presented him with an autographed snooker cue for Bernard to auction at a charity event the comedian was staging at his Manchester nightclub.

* * *

The programmes for the forthcoming cabaret attractions at the Talk continued to include the usual mix of the tried and proven crowd pullers together with some previously untried household names such as Mike and Bernie Winters, Val Doonican and the French heartthrob Sacha Distel.

Ventriloquist Keith Harris was a great hit with the public. He came in one night with what looked like an old box camera that had an antenna taped to it. Part of Keith's act included some banter with his duck Orville with Keith trying to convince his little green friend that he was not real and was in fact only a puppet. The duck was having none of that so finally, and to prove the point that he could not function without him being there, Keith placed Orville on a stool and walked off leaving him alone on the stage. Orville remained motionless for what seemed like an eternity before slowly turning his head in the direction of where Keith had departed. The head then turned back towards the audience and Orville opened his mouth declaring 'He's left me.' The audience gasped.

Keith Harris had converted the old box camera into a remote control and that night Orville became animated for the very first time.

As far back as the sixties my taste in music had been influenced by American recording stars such as Ricky Nelson, Elvis Presley, Bobby Vee and Roy Orbison.

My favourite of them all was Del Shannon and in 1963, after appearing at the Theatre Royal in Norwich, I queued outside in the pouring rain for his autograph which I still have on a black and white photograph to this day. The chance of securing a date during Del's forthcoming British tour was therefore too good an opportunity to miss and I excitedly went to John Fisher to discuss. I was quite deflated when he didn't seem to know who Del Shannon was and therefore assumed that the public wouldn't know either.

In an attempt to get him to change his mind I burst into song with Del's biggest hit *Runaway* but any hope I had of bringing him to Norwich seemed lost when I arrived at the part of the song 'I wonder, I wah wah wah wah wonder.' It was only after other people had convinced John that Del Shannon did actually exist, and they would most certainly come to see him, that the booking was agreed.

The date, as I was certain it would be, was a sell-out and I felt like the boy of sixteen once again when I finally got to meet my hero.

31

During the next four years, from 1976 until the turn of the eighties, both the winter and summer seasons seemed to come and go in rapid succession. Pete and John had left Phoenix but drummer Steve decided to remain and we recruited guitarist Pete Turner together with keyboard player Peter Gordon. That line-up became the mainstay of the band for the remainder of my time with them.

My last four summer seasons with Phoenix were spent working for the two holiday giants, Pontins and Ladbrokes.

At Pontins in Hemsby we were placed in their adult only room which seated about four hundred people and, being the late night drinking and cabaret bar, it was always packed to the brim with regular customers and the overspill from the ballroom after it had closed.

As well as fronting Phoenix, I was also given the role as compere and more or less left to run the evening. There were the usual music sets from the band together with competitions and the visit of a different cabaret entertainer each night. We were fortunate that two of our acts that year were Tony Weston and Carol Lee Scott, both of them great favourites of Pontins.

The following season we switched to Ladbrokes at Caister and our working situation was very much as that we had experienced at Hemsby. The Commodore Club was also an adult only room and situated within the spacious holiday complex. The Commodore had a great atmosphere and, despite competition from the larger family ballroom next door and from a late music bar further down towards the beach, we were always full. Customers piled in for the early evening bingo sessions and kept their seats for the rest of the night's entertainment. Again, as with Hemsby, we were left more or less to our own devices as long as we kept everyone entertained and happy.

Karen Kay was one of the cabaret highlights of our week. She spent many a Wednesday night, prior to her show, sitting in the dressing room, with her hair in rollers, sewing buttons back onto various items of our clothing from which they had become detached.

'Poor little buggers,' she would murmur to herself as she stitched away.

That season whilst at the Commodore we made some great friends amongst the excellent team of Bluecoats.

Jeff Stevenson had previously been to stage school and had appeared in the film *Bugsy Malone*. Surprisingly, considering the job he was doing, he was a quiet and generally shy person and took some coaxing out of his shell. When he eventually did he went on to host TV programmes such as *Knees Up* and *Jumble* as well as touring and opening for Shirley Bassey, Tom Jones, Johnny Mathis and Barry Manilow.

Ian Goode led the team of Bluecoats which included his assistant Irene. The two of them became an item and eventually they married and settled to raise a family in Bournemouth.

After the Commodore Club, Phoenix and I spent our last two summers at Ladbroke's Silver Sands Holiday Centre. The clubhouse there was very large and was the main hub of entertainment for the site. We had a stream of visiting nightly cabaret attractions and the occasional lunchtime special which included the likes of Marty Wilde and Bernie Clifton, both of whom I was always glad to see as I knew a good time would be guaranteed to all.

We created a fun atmosphere at Silver Sands. On Friday lunchtimes we staged our own version of *Cinderella*, a weekly pantomime which was presented with an impressive array of scenery, courtesy of magician Poz who played Buttons. His wife played Cinderella and I was cast as the prince. In one particular scene I had to make my entrance holding Cinder's glass slipper.

'Is that the handsome prince?' Poz enquired when I knocked on the door.

I had secretly prepared a number of different sound effects and the knock on the door would be anything from a doorbell to the chimes of Big Ben. My entrance was just as unpredictable and sometimes I put a smoke bomb in the fireplace and appeared, blackened with soot, from down the chimney. On other occasions, following a loud explosion, I would appear in tattered rags with singed hair and eyebrows or there might suddenly be sounds of gushing water followed by me, soaking wet, wading in wearing snorkel and flippers.

Our Friday pantomime was hilarious and certainly proved a big hit with all the families.

* * *

Included in our nightly entertainment were a wide variety of acts making up our weekly cabaret programme. These included a husband and wife western show that featured lasso twirling, whip cracking and knife throwing.

During the act Trevor, the male half of the duo, called upon a volunteer from the audience to stand in front of a board and have knives thrown at them. At least the request began with the audience until Trevor changed his mind and decided that the volunteer, or victim as he preferred to call them, would be me. This change of tack met with the full approval of the audience, obviously greatly relieved that they were no longer the ones to be selected for the ensuing target practice.

I stood in front of the board with my eyes closed and opened them just in time to notice that Trevor had substituted the knives for an axe. Visions of Charlie from Seaham Harbour suddenly spun through my head as the axe came spinning through the air towards me before embedding itself into the board between my legs. Screams of delight came from the crowd and a stifled squeal of fear from me. Trevor then picked up six knives and very quickly hurled five of them into the area surrounding my head and body. I felt the impact of the sixth knife as it thudded into the board, too close for comfort as the blade nicked a piece of my shirt that had been hanging loose.

'That was great,' said Trevor afterwards. 'The shirt bit worked well, we'll keep that in next week.'

'Next week!' Nobody had mentioned danger money when I took the season. Seven days later and the antics of the previous week were repeated.

'Don't forget to leave enough of your shirt hanging out. And keep still,' Trevor reminded me just before he was due on.

By the time another couple of weeks had passed I was totally immersed into the part and had perfected the look of both surprise and horror when "unexpectedly" called upon to be the volunteer. I removed my jacket to reveal a shirt that now included a large tear in the side and was smeared with tomato ketchup for a blood effect. The audience laughed and I was improvising. I found myself doing what came naturally – I was thinking on my feet and changing the script at will. Whilst basking in my new-found glory I did what I vowed never to do again after the Edentree fiasco at RAF Waddington.

I gave no thought to any possible consequence that my improvisation might have. To me, it felt as if Trevor and I were now the double act, I was the one getting the laughs and all he had to do was throw the knives.

My part in the western act had gotten bigger and now, in addition to my role as the human target, I found myself holding a sheet of newspaper in the air whilst Trevor lashed it in two with his whip. He repeated the action several times and as the paper became smaller he missed and stung the tips of my fingers with the leather. He then moved to the microphone to introduce the knife throwing. What he didn't know was that I had with me a blood capsule and at that point, with Trevor facing the audience and his back to me, I discreetly popped it into my mouth.

That night Trevor's spiel seemed to go on forever and by the time he was ready my bulging cheeks were straining to contain the now rapidly fermenting capsule. I felt the trickle of a warm substance escape from the corner of my mouth and then at long last came the knife that found its mark, agonisingly close to my lose piece of shirt. At that point I spat out the fake blood and slumped forward as if the knife had pinned me to the board.

A cry went up from the audience and Trevor was momentarily in shock at what he thought he'd done. I was summoned before Jack Pound, Ladbrokes director of entertainment. He had received complaints regarding my behaviour but I pleaded that it had all been done in the good name of showmanship. My reasoning did little to appease the situation and I was severely reprimanded.

* * *

On Thursdays, during the main six-week peak period of the summer, there were late night cabaret shows staged in the large ballroom at Ladbrokes main Caister holiday resort. The headlining acts were usually well-known names of the day.

One Thursday I was asked to compere the late show. The support act for that evening was a magician, Steve Bryan, and his assistant Shirley. Part of their act included the Zig Zag Lady, an illusion which consisted of a large box that split into three parts with holes in the top and bottom sections. Shirley's role was to stand in the box and place her head through the upper hole whilst she waved her hand through the bottom one. Steve would then part the middle section creating the illusion that her body had vanished.

The three sections locked together with one door allowing the entire box to open for Shirley to step inside. While the equipment had been left unattended backstage earlier someone had chalked a giant phallus on the door's black interior. The penis had testicles the size of pumpkins and its shaft was the thickness of a sea serpent.

The show began and I introduced Steve Bryan and Shirley. They performed a series of smaller illusions before the time came to present the Zig Zag Lady. Steve wheeled the box to the middle of the floor and, in order to prove that it was empty, he flung the door open. In doing so he revealed the chalked handywork to the audience. With the realisation of what had happened he quickly pushed Shirley inside the box and slammed the door shut.

She poked her head through the upper hole and smiled whilst she pushed a hand, waving a handkerchief, through the lower aperture. Steve Bryan then separated the middle section to rounds of applause. After that he proceeded to restore the three sections before opening the door and attempting to release Shirley as quickly as possible. He was not fast enough however to prevent the audience from another sighting as the phallus once again reared its ugly head, only now it had become smudged and taken on an even more sinister appearance.

I protested my innocence to Jack Pound and insisted that I hadn't been aware of who else had been backstage earlier. I emptied my pockets to prove that I didn't have any chalk and he finally let me go but I was left with the distinct feeling that he didn't believe me.

* * *

For the last week of the season all the winners of the various competitions that had taken place throughout the summer were invited back to compete in the finals. The highlight of the week was the *Miss Ladbrokes* beauty contest. The title carried some national status and consequently, as well as the holiday makers who had been cajoled to take part for a bit of fun, there were the more serious and ambitious girls who had come on holiday with the sole intention of entering the beauty competition.

The majority of winners throughout the season had returned and, after a series of eliminating heats during the course of the week, there were twelve girls remaining. The final itself promised to be a grand occasion – a red carpeted catwalk, supporting a very regal looking throne, had been erected and was lined with flowers. There was also a credible panel of judges chaired by radio DJ David Hamilton.

I once again found myself summoned to Jack Pound's office but this time it was not to be rebuked. After giving assurances that there would be no blood capsules or chalk, I was handed the prestigious job of hosting the beauty contest final.

During the day of the final there was a run-through in order for me to explain the format of events that would take place that night. All of the contestants, some of them chaperoned by mothers and boyfriends, were assembled as I went through the evening's procedure with them.

'When I announce the winner,' I said, taking a girl randomly by the hand and leading her along the catwalk. 'You will then sit on the throne while you are crowned,' and then jokingly added. "And don't forget to cry.'

The evening began and I introduced the judges one by one who took their seats. I then went through the process of introducing and interviewing each of the twelve contestants before each of them paraded up and down the catwalk before finally striking a pose for the photographer. At the end of what was a very long night the judges came to a decision and David Hamilton handed me an envelope containing the number of the winner.

Accompanied by a drum roll I opened the envelope.

'And the winner of *Miss Ladbrokes 1979* is....'

The girl whose hand I had taken during the afternoon run-through burst into tears. Facing a barrage of flashing cameras, she took her place on the throne as the winners sash was draped over her shoulders and the crown placed on her head.

It had gone midnight when I sat in front of Jack Pound in his office.

'Are you absolutely sure?' he said to me.

'Positive,' I replied.

'But the mother says she saw you,' he said.

'She's lying,' was my response.

The mother of one of the other contestants had accused the contest of being fixed claiming that I had shown favouritism to the girl who had won. She even went as far as to say that I had been seen leaving the winner's chalet during the week, which was totally untrue.

'She says she's going to give the story to the Sun,' said Jack. 'And they will want a response.'

'I will deny it,' I said.

Further investigation revealed that the accusations made against me were indeed fabricated and had come from the mouth of a mother who was seemingly desperate to have a beauty queen for a daughter. In the end nobody from the Sun bothered to call me, and nothing was ever published, so the whole sorry business was laid to rest.

32

That summer was my last with Phoenix. It had most certainly been an eventful one, the highlight on Tuesday 19th June when Lyn gave birth to our daughter Natalie. During the days leading up to the birth I had been continually making announcements informing the holiday makers that I was soon to become a dad again. The interest built as more and more people took notice, asking me for regular updates. When Natalie finally arrived there was a tremendous cheer in the room that night and I was presented with a large cigar whilst someone cracked open a bottle of champagne.

Lyn and I were both pleased to have a daughter. It had been seven years since Christian was born and we had made the decision that we wanted to try for another child. During the early stages of the pregnancy neither of us really minded whether we had another boy or a girl but after it was confirmed that we were expecting a daughter, we confessed to each other that in our hearts it was what both of us wanted.

***

After Natalie had come into our lives we both decided that there would be no more children and, as the easiest option, I decided to have a vasectomy. I made an appointment to see a urologist who booked me to into a private clinic to undergo the procedure a few weeks later.

The day of the operation finally came round and I arrived at the nursing home early one morning as instructed. The door opened and I was greeted by a face I vaguely recognised.

'Oh hiya Brian, come on in. When I saw the name on the list I wondered if it might be you.'

Diane was the girlfriend of one of the members of a band that worked for Norwich Artistes. I remembered he once told me that she was a nurse but I had no idea she worked at that particular nursing home. She took me into a room where there was a gown waiting for me and she asked me to take off my clothes and slip into it whilst she completed the formalities of the paperwork. She then proceeded with an inspection of my bits and pieces to ensure that I had come suitably prepared. There came a knock on the door and she looked up as a jovial looking orderly walked in.

'Oh hiya Colin,' chirped Diane. 'This is Brian. Brian this is Colin,' she announced.

'Hi Brian,' replied Colin. 'Thanks Diane, I'll handle it from here.'

Colin's mannerisms, together with a small earring that he wore, left me with little doubt as to his sexual preferences. I wasn't quite sure what he intended to "handle" exactly but I felt quite relaxed about the whole thing, after all we were already on first name terms. In the short space of time that it took for him to lead me along a hallway and into the small operating theatre, Colin had practically told me his life story, including his time before entering the medical profession, when he was a dresser for the actor Derek Nimmo.

Inside the theatre the serious business began and it was back to strict formalities as I was reintroduced to Mr Urologist. He explained what would happen during the vasectomy and said that it was all very simple and straight-forward – two small incisions into the scrotum followed by the removal of a small section of tubing and before you knew it, Bob's your uncle or, with a careless slip of his scalpel, it could well have been Brian's your auntie.

'But first,' he said. 'I'll just pop an injection into your testicles.'

My backside instantly retreated as far away from the needle as it possibly could and had embedded itself into the paper towelling that covered the table I was lying on.

'Just a tiny prick,' he informed me – he really did say that. I must admit that I smiled at his comment before my mood quickly changed when I felt a sharp jab and the thought "bollocks" came into my head. After that there was nothing more than a dull ache and in a matter of minutes I was done.

I bid my farewell to Diane as I left the clinic not long after.

'And remember to wear swimming trunks or tight under-pants to ease the swelling,' she called to me at the front door. Her advice had carried on the wind and found the ear of a passing cyclist who turned his head with interest in our direction.

'I'll tell John that I've seen you,' she said as she closed the door.

A few weeks passed by and it was time for me to provide the first sample as proof of my impending infertility. I shut myself in the bathroom, alone with my thoughts and a small plastic bottle. My vasectomy had been performed privately and I had been given an address of a house to where I had to make the delivery.

'Just put the bottle in the envelope and stick it through the letterbox,' I was told.

Such a simple instruction but, as I approached the road, I realised that I couldn't remember the number of the house. The last thing I wanted to do was to post it through the wrong door so I stopped the car and considered my options. There was nothing else for it, I would have to return home and recheck the house number, and whilst I was there?

I held the container up to the light and inspected its contents. I shook it and the pitifully shallow amount of semen inside swirled lazily around the bottom.

'That's not much of a specimen,' I thought. 'I can do better than that.'

So there you have it – a readymade situation comedy all nicely scripted and rolled into one. Real life experiences can be so much funnier than just telling jokes and the tale of my vasectomy soon found its rightful place into my stage act.

33

The Lord Giveth and The Lord Taketh Away. Little more than eight months after Natalie had come into the world Chic Applin departed it.

Chic had been so determined to get our new business venture started as soon as possible that he called one day to say that he had been to view offices. Whilst David and I were content to remain at the Talk we went along with Chic's proposal and, after seeing the premises, we agreed that they were ideal. All that was needed now was for us to sign the rental agreement.

* * *

Joe Butler was a builder and property developer who had undertaken an extensive redevelopment of the Town House Hotel. The hotel was delightfully located at the river's edge and so much was its appeal that Joe decided to keep it himself and operate it as a family business. He planned to present weekly dinner dances with cabaret and contacted us to ask if we would provide the entertainment.

The opening night was by invite only. The three of us, David, Chic and I, together with our respective partners, were included on the guest list and Chic's band, fronted by bassist Don Shepherd, provided the music. The evening was coming to an end when Chic decided to join the band on stage for the final number. Halfway through the song *Show Me the Way to Go Home* he collapsed suffering from a brain haemorrhage and was rushed to hospital.

For the next seven days Chic laid in a bed fighting for his life. In the early hours one morning I suddenly awoke sensing that something was wrong, I drove to the hospital where Chic's wife Jill was waiting. I was told that Chic hadn't long left and I was allowed in to see him. I talked to him and, although he was unable to respond, I felt sure that he knew I was there. He finally slipped away at 4.30 a.m.

It is impossible for anyone to try and put themselves in someone else's shoes when such a tragic event such as a family death occurs. People tend to react in all manner of different ways when they are grieving and in deep shock. After Jill had said goodbye to her husband for the last time she asked if I would clean out the contents of his car. Chic was not the most methodical of people and much of his business was contained on bits of paper stored in the boot. Three hours later I had removed and filed every piece of paperwork.

Chic Applin was only fifty-two years old and his untimely death proved just how cruel life can be. He left behind a wife, together with a young son Nick and daughter Michelle. Michelle was already showing an interest in music whilst Chic had expressed feelings that David Clayton might one day take Nicholas under his wing as a DJ.

The funeral itself was a small and private affair but, because Chic was such a well known figure, David and I felt it appropriate that we plan a memorial service in his name. The problem we had was that, with the large numbers anticipated who would want to attend, where could we hold it? We eventually managed to arrange the service at Norwich Cathedral and hundreds of people turned out to honour the man.

The celebration of Chic's life was conducted with the utmost reverence, so much so that the Bishop of Norwich congratulated us afterwards saying that he had initial reservations about a show business ceremony to which I could not resist 'Oh ye of little faith.'

That particular story of 'Oh ye of little faith' did the rounds so often afterwards that there were people, all claiming ownership of my comment, who were still quoting it back to me months later.

* * *

When everything had finally been laid to rest David and I had our hands full. The venture with Chic that had been planned would not now go ahead but we were determined to secure his business for Jill and her children – there were already rivals waiting in the wings eager to pick away at what they could for themselves. We contacted all the venues and told them that the forthcoming summer season would go ahead as planned. We knew the acts that Chic had been intending to book and sent them their contracts whilst at the same time fending off those who falsely claimed that they had been promised work. The task was so great that we took on a secretary to ease the workload.

The planning and preparation had all gone well and everything appeared to have stabilised. Jill Applin announced the amalgamation of Chic's agency with Norwich Artistes and the press turned up to take pictures and report the news.

Sometime later we received a phone call from Jill saying that she wanted to come and see us. She showed up late in the afternoon after having been out with Chris North. Jill appeared to be tipsy and I suspect that she may have needed a drop of Dutch courage before telling us that she had changed her mind about joining Norwich Artistes. She said that she intended on running the Chic Applin Agency herself, alongside Chris. She even went so far as to say that it would have been what Chic wanted which we knew was not the case. Her turnabout was a very bitter pill to swallow.

Other than attending social events with her husband, Jill had never bothered herself in Chic's business and Chris North had no real experience of running an entertainment agency. Consequently it was not long before things started to go wrong for them and we began to receive calls from their venues asking if Norwich Artistes could take over their bookings. Almost inevitably Chic Applin's agency folded soon after.

We asked our newly recruited secretary Gill if she could work longer hours to assist with the additional business that we had taken on.

34

I was now in my sixth year at the Talk and it felt as if the best times were behind us. The venue was just about managing to hold its own but a new and different type of humour had become fashionable and competition was beginning to bite. Alternative comedians were proving popular with the younger generation and the general absence of mainstream variety entertainment meant there were very few new acts coming through with appeal to an older and more cabaret minded audience. We mainly had to rely on the tried and proven names.

Through all of this however, there were still one or two memorable moments that helped lift the spirit.

During a Christmas season lunchtime show, when I was on stage performing the Johnny Mathis number *When a Child is Born*, Lyn had turned up with babe-in-arms Natalie who, seeing me on stage, proceeded to crawl the entire length of the dance floor to get to me. Natalie's timing was perfect as I picked her up in my arms just as the song came to an end.

Bernie Clifton was always a joy to work with and forever the joker. He had been booked for two nights and on the first night it came to the part in his act when he awarded the prize of a brand new moped to a member of the audience. Upon this cue, a mop head would then be flung onto the stage. On that particular Friday night there just happened to be a moped on the premises and when Bernie announced the prize I kicked the machine into life and rode it out onto the cabaret floor. Smoke and fumes billowed from its exhaust and into the chicken-in-the-basket eating public sitting at front tables.

When I went on stage to bring him off at the end of his act Bernie and I had some repartee regarding the next day's FA Cup Final between Arsenal and Manchester United. Bernie was convinced that Arsenal would win but I said that a Manchester United victory was a certainty and offered to show my backside on stage the next night if proven wrong. It was all said in jest and in nothing more than a light-hearted moment.

The following afternoon Arsenal were two goals up and it seemed as if Bernie would be proven right until Manchester United hit back with two goals in the last five minutes. It looked like the game would go into extra time until Alan Sunderland popped up with a very late Arsenal winner.

In the evening Bernie Clifton called for the brand new moped and I tossed out the mop head accordingly. He then went into his *Desert Song* routine – complete with the cat on his shoulder, spraying water over the crowd. He featured a twelve-foot long rubber shark during *Mack the Knife* and rode his mischievous ostrich around the floor. He finished his act to yells for more and I was about to offer the encore when Bernie held me by the arm and quietened the audience.

He then explained what had happened the previous night regarding our Cup Final predictions and told the people about my pledge should Manchester United lose. Fortunately I had anticipated that Bernie Clifton was not one to pass up a moment such as this and I was prepared.

Written in lipstick was HE on my left buttock and LP on the other. I turned my back to the audience and lowered my trousers to reveal the word HELP on my backside.

* * *

The winds of change were certainly making their presence felt. In 1980 BBC Radio Norfolk began broadcasting in Norwich and David Clayton progressed from local hospital radio to a regular weekly slot on the station. He also had a foot in the door, both as a continuity announcer and presenter, with Anglia and BBC television.

I too felt the need for a fresh challenge and decided to leave Phoenix and continue working solo as a vocal and comedy entertainer. I had assumed that this move would involve nothing more than a few local bookings and certainly had not anticipated the opportunities and workload that would follow.

Wembley bound 1963: (l-r) Ron Davies (Norwich City & Wales), Peter Batch, Barry Futter, David Smith, Brian Storey-Smith, Brian Wigg and me.

Influence in 1966: (l-r) Barry Wilkinson, me, Nick Day and Derek Pickering.

Phil Beevis who made it all possible. Without him there would
be no story.

Edentree: (l-r) Roger Cooke, me, Nick MacCartney, Mick Elliott and
Pete Holmes.

Edentree performing our Bachelors routine during the
Opportunity Knocks audition.

Christian as a street urchin in BBC's *Woman in White*

The Talk 1975: (l-r) Steve Goodrum (Phoenix), me, Warren Mitchell, John Tubby (Phoenix) and Karen Kay.

Phoenix at the Talk in 1976: (l-r) Steve Goodrum, Pete Turner, me, Peter Gordon.

"When a Child is Born." Me with Natalie at the Talk Christmas 1979.

Me clowning on stage at the Talk with Bernie Clifton.

A stitch in time. Ronnie Fisher to the rescue with needle and thread before an evening show at The Talk.

Backstage antics at Silver Sands. (l-r) Chic Applin, Tony (compere), me, Bernie Clifton and David Clayton.

35

Mac Mackay, the Commercial Manager at Norwich City Football Club, called one day to say that ATV were planning a new series called *Up For The Cup* and had asked if Norwich City would be interested in putting forward a team of entertainers to represent the club. The team had to consist of four acts that would compete head-to-head against other acts representing different football teams. It was basically a variety show designed on a football knock-out basis with the winner being decided on which team had scored the most points at the end of the show. The judges were to be football managers and club supporters would make up the studio audience. Mac asked if Norwich Artistes would put the team together for the programme.

David and I of course relished the challenge but who should we choose to represent Norwich City? With a national TV show up for grabs we had much talent eager to participate and were spoilt for choice but the four acts we eventually decided on were Fresh Aire, in the music slot, comedian Lew Lewis, speciality double act Trevillion and Nine and mind reader Graham P Jolley.

The host for *Up For the Cup* was David Hamilton. Norwich City's first appearance on the programme was against Sunderland and both teams were cheered on in the studio by supporters decked out in a sea of yellow and green and red and black. The quality of the acts representing Sunderland was high as expected but Norwich came through triumphant.

In the semi-final we found ourselves competing against Charlton Athletic, whose team included singer Maggie Moone,

TV debutant Bobby Davro and Jim Bowen. I was annoyed that Jim was representing Charlton and had jokingly announced that I would put in a transfer request for him. Despite such a rich vein of talent against us we matched them all the way but were finally beaten by a solitary point.

It was not until the programme had ended and the studio audience were filing out that Lew Lewis began arguing with one of the production team. The scores for each team had been displayed on two flip boards and Lew insisted that, after we had won a particular round, David Hamilton had flicked the points over to Charlton by mistake. Had that not happened we would have had the higher score and made the final.

Lew was incensed and threatened to expose ATV for cheating. My mind immediately went back to the time at Caister and the *Miss Ladbroke's* final when there had been similar accusations of fixing. David Hamilton had also been present that night and I began to think that maybe he was a jinx.

The exchanges in the studio became more and more heated – by now Sadie Nine had begun to remonstrate with some of the Charlton supporters. I decided to stay out of the way and retreated to the Green Room where I joined Jim Bowen for some peace and quiet. While we were there, Jim was approached and told that ATV wanted to talk to him about a new idea they had for a game show – something to do with darts.

* * *

My association with Norwich City continued to grow when double glazing firm Poll and Withey became the club sponsors. The football club was targeted by a music company who had composed a new club song called *See the Canaries*. Norwich had initially shown an interest in the song and I was asked to travel to the company's studio in Grimsby to record the vocal track. Instead of being rallying and inspiring, as a football song should be, the lyrics were no match for the other great soccer anthems of our time. Needless to say nothing more ever came of it and the idea was eventually dropped.

(Verse 1)

I'm saving all my money for every Saturday...
To buy me a ticket to see Norwich City play.
They play a class of football away or at home...
Running down the touchline to score another goal.
(Chorus)
See the Canaries down at Carrow Road...
See the Canaries put on a first-class show...
See the Canaries their playing is so neat...
See the Canaries a better team I've yet to meet

And so on.

Poll and Withey then came up with their own Christmas song. On Boxing Day I stood, heavily disguised in full Father Christmas costume, complete with a flowing white beard, on the centre circle at Carrow Road. There were twenty-six thousand people in the stadium that afternoon to hear my rendition of...

Good King Wenceslas last looked out of the ultimate window ..."

'Saw you at Carrow Road yesterday,' someone remarked after.

My next appearance on the hallowed turf was much more enjoyable. I had previously played in a couple of games for Radio Norfolk's football team and was invited to be in the side to play against a Norwich City All Stars eleven. The match was part of the celebration of the opening of the new stand after the previous enclosure had been destroyed by a fire at the ground. Our team, captained by City legend Terry Allcock, was a mixture of Radio Norfolk and ex-Norwich players and we found ourselves up against a Norwich side which included some current first team members who had over one hundred international caps between them. Being on the same pitch as Wales' David Jones and England's Martin Peters, who was pinging the ball around for fun, was a great experience. Despite a 4-1 defeat we gave a good account of ourselves.

36

My cabaret work was keeping me busy. The weekend bookings generally took me into clubs as far afield as Bedfordshire and Northamptonshire whilst the majority of my midweek bookings were as the compere for Ladies Hen Nights throughout the Home Counties. Slotted in amongst all this I also had theatre dates alongside Max Bygraves and Frankie Vaughan as well as hosting Rock n' Roll package shows which featured famous groups from the sixties.

My first summer season as a solo act included three nights a week for Pontins on the West Sussex coast. Lennie Peters was also appearing on the same circuit and, during the main season, Bob Monkhouse came in alongside us and starred in one of the resort's ballrooms. After the season it was back to the club circuit together with a welcome break of two weeks abroad for Pontinental at their Ten Bel resort in southern Tenerife where I was allowed to take Christian with me.

With me being away so much, and David becoming more and more involved with radio, it was a pressurised period for Norwich Artistes. To combine both our work schedules we were constantly juggling balls in the air, with a number of them falling into Gill's lap. Consequently she found herself taking on an even greater workload which she seemed more than happy to do.

* * *

Whilst working for Pontins that year I became friendly with Bryn, one of the Entertainment Managers. He suggested that I would do well in South Wales.

I myself was not too sure. It was a known fact that the welcome in the hillside, offered by the Welsh, did not always extend to English entertainers.

Clive Webb was a very zany magician who featured some very loud explosives in his act. There had been an occasion when Phoenix appeared with him and, unannounced, he detonated a dustbin that happened to be positioned directly behind Steve the drummer. The impact of the explosion, not only showered Steve in fifty years of muck and dust that had been dislodged from the rafters of the old building, it also caused him partial deafness for the best part of a week.

Clive Webb was appearing at a social club in a South Wales mining village. The venue had, over a few recent weeks, presented a number of English acts, none of whom had gone down particularly well with the audience. During his first spot, Clive set off an almighty explosion at the very moment that a senior member of the club, carrying a tray of drinks, happened to be passing by the front of the stage. The story goes that the senior member instantly dropped down dead but the truth of the matter was that he suffered no more than an urgent need for a change of underwear.

The club instantly paid Clive off and sent him on his way home before he could fulfil his second spot. The following week the concert chairman announced that the venue would not be booking any more English acts in the foreseeable future.

'Instead tonight' he said 'We have Gwyneth from the local Presbyterian church who will sing for us – but first, a game of bingo. He switched on the bingo machine and BOOM!!

Clive Webb had detonated the machine.

* * *

When my summer season had finished Bryn arranged a week of bookings for me in social clubs throughout South Wales. I stayed at his house that week and I was at my final venue on the Saturday night when Bryn called asking if I would do an extra show at another venue later that same evening. I was looking forward to getting home but Bryn had been a very hospitable host and so I agreed. He told me that the venue was the Double Diamond nightclub in Caerphilly.

I finished at the social club and headed over the hills and down the valley towards Caerphilly. Some of the roads were narrow, unlit and badly signposted and after a while it began to rain. I lost my way a couple of times and it was late when I finally reached a building that looked like a large warehouse. The car park was full and I could see a light shining from an open door. The door led into a dressing room.

'At last, thank goodness,' remarked the person who had been anticipating my arrival. 'I'll get the band.' Bryn had mentioned that the venue had a resident seven-piece band and I quickly talked them through my music as I got ready.

It was all such a rush. I hadn't been in the building more than half-an-hour when I found myself standing behind a closed curtain. I could hear the compere quietening the audience and then came my introduction. The band struck up my opening number as the curtains parted and I walked out to over a thousand people. The gods were certainly with me that night and I went on to have one of the best shows I can remember. The audience was so responsive and when I finished I was called back for more – I had been on stage for over an hour and the crowd were standing and clapping.

The manager of the Double Diamond then stepped forward to the microphone.

He apologised for the unfortunate situation that the club had found itself in earlier that day and thanked me for stepping in at the last minute. Another round of applause came from the audience.

'Tonight you came to see a Starr,' he continued. 'And I think you will agree with me that you've seen one!'

Freddie Starr had originally been booked that night and had cancelled at the last minute. The Double Diamond had been phoning around for a replacement and Bryn had come to the rescue. The people who had bought tickets and turned up were told what had happened and were given the option of a full refund or a reduced admission if they decided to stay. It seemed that most of them had remained.

The anticipated long and tiring journey home simply flew by as I re-lived the moment over and over again.

37

In 1982 Billy Fury announced that he was planning to tour again. Billy had been a major recording star in the sixties but had not made any live appearances for a number of years due to ill health which had dogged him since childhood. He was now considered fit enough to undertake some dates to promote his new record and I was asked if there was anywhere I would be able to place him. Of course I immediately thought of the Talk but John Fisher was not interested.

He thought Billy Fury wouldn't pull due to the fact that he had been off the scene for so long. I told John that I felt exactly the opposite – the fact that he hadn't performed in public for a number of years would bring the people out to see him. John still wasn't convinced and, after a verse of *Halfway to Paradise* from me had failed to get him to change his mind, I turned to plan B.

Barry Rose was a local entrepreneur who had founded his own pioneering travel agency called Go Continental. Barry was very much a showman at heart and when I mentioned Billy Fury to him he immediately agreed to take a date. A Monday in October at the Norwood Rooms was arranged and John Fisher could not believe it.

'A Monday!' he said. 'You must be mad. You won't get people coming out on a Monday.' The Monday night came and over nine hundred people turned up to witness the return of the legend.

From the moment that he made his entrance it was quite obvious that Billy Fury was not in the best of health but he managed to work his way through a forty-minute set and afterwards the people queued to meet him. The show that night was videoed by Barry Rose who later lent out the cassette tape of the recording. Barry couldn't remember who he had given it to and the video was never returned. What would have been a cherished piece of pop memorabilia was gone.

***

The morning after his appearance at the Norwood Rooms John Fisher asked for the first available date on Billy Fury for the Talk and I booked him to appear on Saturday 29th January 1983. Billy sold out very quickly, John was very happy and I couldn't resist an 'I told you so.' When January arrived people were still asking if there were any more tickets available. There then came the dreadful and untimely news.

Returning from a recording session in the early hours of Friday 28th January, Billy Fury had collapsed at his London home. His personal manager, Tony Read, found him unconscious the next morning and Billy was rushed to St Mary's hospital in Paddington where he died later that afternoon. He was forty-two years old.

Tony Read phoned me first thing on the Friday morning with the initial news that Billy had been taken into hospital and would not be able to appear on Saturday. I braced myself and made the call to John Fisher.

'Fucking typical,' was John's reply which, to this day, I have never quite understood. John had clearly underestimated the gravity of Billy Fury's condition and I would like to think that his comment was a spur of the moment thing, and born out of the anger that he had a full house and no star attraction. By now the media had broken the news and throughout the morning there were more and more people phoning the Talk to ask what was happening on Saturday.

Where to begin in finding a suitable replacement at such a late hour? I turned to Marty Wilde and as luck would have it he was available. Marty was very much a firm favourite at the

Talk but he was not too keen on coming when I told him the circumstances that we found ourselves in.

'The place will be full of Billy's fans,' he said. 'They won't be coming to see me.' I reminded Marty that he and Billy both came from that same golden musical era.

'If they are fans of Billy's music they will also be fans of yours' I assured him and thankfully Marty agreed to come.

The following night, Marty Wilde and the Wildcats delivered their usual high-octane performance and Marty even included a couple of Billy's hits in tribute to the passing of his friend.

It was hard to accept that, just twelve weeks earlier, Billy Fury had stood on stage at the Norwood Rooms. One of his hits he sang that night was *I'd Never Find Another You* which included the opening line 'Don't ever worry that I'd leave you.' How very wrong those words turned out to be.

38

'It's only a few drinks and some nibbles but you are quite welcome to join us,' said Mollie Sugden backstage at the Theatre Royal.

Mollie, fresh from her success as Mrs Slocombe in the television sitcom *Are You Being Served,* was touring the country in a play. Ron Davies, who was best remembered in the late sixties for his role as PC Doug Roach in *Z Cars,* was also in the production. Ron was also a singer and, when he arrived in Norwich, one of his first ports of call was the office of Norwich Artistes to introduce himself. He invited me along to see the play and I turned up on the night that happened to be Mollie Sugden's birthday. She was a most charming and hospitable lady and invited us all back to her hotel for a small celebration.

***

I got to know the actor Bill Maynard from his association with local entrepreneur Neville Downing. It was a rags to riches story for Neville, who began his business life trading from the back of a van and ended up owning properties along Prince of Wales Road. As his property portfolio grew some of us renamed the road Downing Street.

Neville was very much a joker and it was reflected by the nature of his business. He sold practical jokes – itching and sneezing powder, fart cushions, fake dog poo and magic wands – all available at his shop which he named Magic Products. He also supplied merchandise, such as mugs and key rings, to showbiz clients who included Jimmy Jones and Ian and Jeanette Tough, better known as the Krankies. Bill Maynard had also placed orders with Neville for items baring the inscription "Magic," which was a catchword he became known for during his successful comedy TV series *Oh No, it's Selwyn Froggitt!*

Bill was in Norwich for the Christmas season starring in the pantomime *Jack and the Beanstalk*. Playing principal boy alongside him was Melanie Peck, the daughter of the acclaimed actress Jennifer Wilson and actor/producer Brian Peck. Melanie was a singer and when the pantomime finished she formed a vocal duo with her friend Amanda Green. They called themselves Blondessence and the two tall leggy blondes enjoyed a short but successful career, especially in the Far-East where they proved particularly popular. I represented the act for a while.

***

David and I continued to broaden our personal horizons and as a result we were both spending less time in the office with Gill. David had committed himself to more radio airtime and my cabaret work was taking me all over the place.

I made appearances in Germany, with one trip in particular proving quite gruelling. I was part of a touring show that had been arranged by impresario Mike Powell. The show also included singer Eve Bridger, vocal guitarist Nicky Walker, ventriloquist Brian Chamberlin and Trefor Thomas and John Marshall, better known as Twice as Nice. We travelled in two vans that also carried the sound and lighting equipment and our work schedule took us to UK and US military bases in both East and West Berlin.

Having arrived in Zeebrugge on the Harwich ferry we disembarked and travelled from Belgium to Bielefeld in Germany, more than three hundred miles and five hours later. The town was the halfway point to our final destination and we stopped for a short break at the home of Chris, an ex-serviceman who had been responsible for putting the tour together. From Bielefeld we then journeyed on to complete the remaining two hundred and fifty miles arriving at Checkpoint Charlie, the border wall crossing that divided the city of Berlin. At the crossing we were eyed suspiciously by leather-coated soldiers. One peered through the window of the van I had been driving and caught a glimpse of Brian Chamberlin, with his hair flattened to one side and a small square black stick-on moustache covering his top lip. The guard was clearly not amused at Brian's uncannily lifelike impression of Adolf Hitler and, giving me a prod in the back with the barrel of his rifle, I was handed our documents and ordered back into the van.

From Checkpoint Charlie, we finally arrived at the Montgomery Barracks in Kladow which was to be our home while in Berlin. Every morning around 6.00 a.m. we were woken up by gunfire in what appeared to be a psychological battle between the Americans, Russians, Germans, French and probably every other nation with a presence in the region. I was convinced that the ritual was little more than a military exercise to see who could make the loudest bang.

In Berlin we entertained both the British and American troops and between the shows we found time to take in the sights. We saw Spandau prison, then the home of its solitary inmate Rudolph Hess, and we also visited the Brandenburg Gate and the Reichstag building, which housed the German parliament. At the Berlin Wall, the pain and suffering of those who had tried to cross over from East to West, and who had been shot and fallen, was evident for all to see.

* * *

Back home in Norwich the plight of a baby girl came to my attention. Caron had been born with only one arm and the newspaper article reported that her parents were organising fund-raising events for her to have a prosthetic limb fitted.

A number of us local entertainers decided to help and we put on a charity show at the Talk to start the fund ball rolling. We then decided that we would form our own charity and we called ourselves Anglian Charities Theatrical Society, or ACTS for short. We spread the word far and wide about Caron and soon there were sponsored events, both here in the UK and abroad, contributing to our charity. There were so many generous people out there and it was not long before we had enough money, not only for Caron's prosthetic arm, but also for the upgrades she would need as she grew and developed into adulthood.

We still had money left over and, after we had made an unsuccessful attempt to buy a kidney dialysis machine for a local hospital, it was agreed that we would distribute the remaining funds towards local worthy causes such as for Robert, a young boy struck down with muscular dystrophy. Our contribution helped reconstruct the interior of the bungalow where he lived and allowed him easier wheelchair access.

We also donated to the Clare School, a mixed day Foundation School for pupils of ages ranging from three years to late teens who had physical and sensory needs. The school wanted to provide an environment that celebrated and encouraged success and achievement and we were pleased that our donation helped to build a raised garden area that could be nurtured by handicapped pupils in wheelchairs.

David and I went to the school to present the cheque and I was later given a cutting from *The Brian Russell Rose* – a yellow rose that had been cultivated in the newly constructed garden and subsequently named after me.

39

I returned to the Talk to compere a series of Sunday night talent competitions. The shows attracted local sponsorship and proved popular with the family audiences who turned out to support the acts competing. There had been a number of such events staged during my time there and some of the contestants had gone on to enjoy successful careers.

They included comedy magician Kevin Woolley, musician Ian Larkin and singers Patrina Jons, Kerry Andrews, Julie Bunn, Sadie Jones, Denise Summers and Sue Brookes as well as drummer Steve Barney who became the percussionist for a number of acts, including the Sugarbabes and Annie Lennox.

***

Locally, one of my favourite places that I enjoyed working at was owned by Mr Loucas. He was a very gracious gentleman who came from Greece and his restaurant, the Savoy, on Prince of Wales Road, was a very popular eating place. It hosted a five-piece resident band and presented a weekly cabaret as well as traditional Greek nights of plate smashing and belly-dancing. Neville Downing's La Valbon nightclub, situated above his Magic Products premises, was just a few doors down from the Savoy and it was convenient for me, as the booker for both venues, to double up the cabaret acts. They would finish at the Savoy just past 11.00 p.m. and then make a mad dash down the road for a midnight spot at La Valbon.

I was appearing at the Savoy one night when I noticed a man sitting by himself at a far corner table. His face seemed familiar but I couldn't place it. It was only after I had finished my act that the penny dropped and I realised who he was.

The Hollywood film star James Stewart was a veteran of the US Army Air Force and had been stationed in Norfolk for a while during the Second World War. He was back in the county, along with other US veterans, to revisit airfields where military operations had taken place. He happened to be staying at a hotel just down the road from the Savoy.

On another occasion, when I was appearing there, I saw a face that I instantly recognised. Actor Telly Savalas, star of the seventies TV series *Kojak* was in Norwich filming an episode of *Tales of the Unexpected* for Anglia Television. Telly and Mr Loucas knew each other from way back in Greece and had been friends for a very long time. That night there was a press photographer on hand to capture the moment of their reunion.

* * *

My New Year's Eve in 1982 was spent in the Brighton and Hove district of Sussex. I had originally been booked to appear at two venues in the area but, as the date drew nearer, additional shows were added and the two venues eventually became four.

The evening actually began for me late afternoon when I had to set up sound equipment in two of the places that did not have any. During the evening I shuffled from one venue to another, being shoved into slots between the general merry-making and Auld Lang Syne, and it had gone 1.00 a.m. by the time I finished my fourth and final spot. I then had to return to the two venues to collect the PA systems I had set up earlier in the day. Dawn was breaking by the time everything had finally been sorted but, although accommodation had been booked for me at the Grand Hotel, I was past sleep. All I wanted to do was get back to Norwich.

During that long drive home I became quite tired and morose as my mind drifted. I began to take stock of my life.

Nothing much had really changed from how it had been during my time on the road with Edentree. I had left the band because I didn't want to live that kind of lifestyle anymore but it hadn't ended and I was doing more or less the same as before, only now I was doing it on my own. I was also aware that my responsibilities were now far greater having two young children to take care of – Christian had just turned ten and Natalie was three years old.

How had my life managed to slip back to what it had been eleven years before? Quite simply it had because I had allowed it to. After my time with Phoenix, going solo had seemed the most natural thing for me to do but I had not anticipated the amount of work and the extra time and travel that it would involve.

My thoughts then turned to Lyn. Although we had known each other for a long time I wondered if we really knew each other at all, there seemed to be a void between us. During the thirteen years or more that we had been married, much of that time had been spent apart and we had in practice been leading two separate lives. Did I care for her? Yes of course I cared; I had deep feelings for her but then I asked myself did I really love her, or indeed, did she really love me? I could not be sure of the answer either way.

What I did realise however was that I had to start playing my part if our marriage was to stand any chance of surviving.

In February 1983, I had been re-booked once again for Pontinental in Tenerife and saw this as an opportunity for Lyn and I to have some quality time on our own and perhaps, in doing so, become closer again. With Christian and Natalie safely in the care of Lyn's mother, the two of us spent a fortnight together in the warm early season sunshine.

After returning to Norfolk, refreshed from the break and with March and April very much local regarding my immediate cabaret work, I was looking forward to spending more time at home. There was only one run of dates that I had to be away for.

I was booked for a week at the Variety Bar in Skegness, beginning on the bank holiday weekend at the end of May.

40

The Variety Bar, situated on the promenade in Skegness, was a magnet of entertainment for the visiting holidaymakers. They thronged in for the lunchtime and evening sessions that were provided by the resident organist and drummer and local comedian and compere Sid Dennis. As well as the resident team, there were various cabaret acts that appeared on a weekly basis. The bank holiday week was an especially busy schedule for me with seven shows at the Variety Bar and an additional three performances at various holiday parks along the Skegness coastline.

My opening spot was on the Sunday lunchtime and when I arrived in the morning I discovered that I was sharing the week with a girl singer from Newcastle who was due to arrive later for the evening show. I received an appreciative response from the audience which was a good way to start as Roy Tipper, the agent who had booked me, was watching. Afterwards I went for a wander into the town. When I returned to the Variety Bar, the organist and drummer were in the dressing room, along with the girl singer, having a run-through of her music. I burst in rather noisily and unexpectedly and promptly received a sharp rebuff for interrupting. I offered my apologies and quickly left.

'That's Norwich Artistes,' Sid Dennis explained to Denise Morrell. She had never heard of Norwich Artistes and was clearly not impressed with me. I was wearing a white leather jacket which probably contributed to her opinion that I was just another flash southerner!

I watched Denise on stage that night and was smitten. She had thick dark coiffured hair and was dressed in a full length gold outfit. She looked stunning and proceeded to win the crowd over with her singing and cutting edge humour. As I sat amongst the audience I felt myself attracted towards her in a way that I had never felt before.

If there is such a thing as love at first sight then that night for me was surely the moment. As the week wore on a mutual attraction gradually developed between us until Saturday finally arrived and we had to say our goodbyes. I asked for her phone number – Denise later admitted that she had considered giving me a wrong number thinking that maybe I would not bother to call her.

Thankfully she didn't.

* * *

The following six months saw my life turned well and truly upside down.

Firstly David Clayton dropped the bombshell that he had been offered a daily programme with Radio Norfolk as a full-time broadcaster. It was something that he had wanted for a while and now a position with the BBC had finally come his way, under no circumstances was he going to turn it down. It was a huge blow but with sufficient notice, and with Gill remaining in the office, there was time for us to take over his workload and complete a smooth transition.

At about the same time Ray Aldous decided to seek pastures new and the Talk was taken over by a business consortium consisting of Pat McNamee an accountant, Tim Enright who had previously been involved with racing cars at Lotus and Silvio Markovic, a Yugoslavian financial adviser. An ex-publican called Ryan became the new manager.

They called me to a meeting and outlined their intentions of continuing to operate the business until the end of the year when they would close for a few months while extensive alterations took place. They intended raising the profile of the Talk by presenting bigger names on a regular basis with an in-house floorshow supporting the headline acts. I was assured that my situation would not change regarding use of the office, or my role as the booking agent for the venue.

I set about putting down ideas for the floorshow, which was to be a forty-five minute programme of song, dance and comedy. The plan was to change the content of the show on a monthly basis which would necessitate rehearsal of new material at the same time as performing the current production.

We already had the right band in place with Fresh and we needed dancers. I made contact with a local dance school that was able to provide a troupe of six girls as well as a guarantee of backup in the event of any of the girls becoming unavailable. I said that I was happy to return as the compere but what were we to do about a resident girl singer? Ryan said he wanted to investigate various options before making a decision.

There were not many days when Denise and I did not speak by phone. I felt that there was something special happening between us but she had her life up north and, with such a distance between us, it was impossible to imagine anything ever developing further.

* * *

Not long after David's departure, Gill broke the news that she too was leaving.

She told me that she intended forming her own entertainment agency and wanted me to sell her Norwich Artistes – she even suggested that if I did not she would be able to take it anyway. The extra responsibility that she had been given had played very conveniently into Gill's hands – she had become the name and the voice that people recognised. David's leaving, and now my own situation, had provided her with sufficient ammunition and the confidence to culture the impression with clients that Norwich Artistes was on the verge of collapse but that she was there to take over.

The office that had once been vibrant with the ringing of telephones and sounds of voices was suddenly strangely quiet. There was now only me and, as I stared across the room at two empty desks, I felt anger inside. I was not prepared to stand by and let someone take from me what had been such a major part of my life for so long. I decided to fight back.

The stillness was broken by the sound of a phone ringing.

'Hello Norwich Artistes,' I answered. 'No, I'm Brian Russell. Gill doesn't work here anymore.'

41

I had been booking girl singers into a casino on Portugal's Algarve and there was a vacant slot that needed filling.

I called Denise and asked if she wanted to go to Portugal for three weeks at the end of November. The date she would be due to arrive back in England coincided with hypnotist Tony Sands being booked at the Talk and it just so happened that I needed a support act for that night. I told Denise that I would collect her from Heathrow airport and bring her to Norwich for the show and it could be arranged for Tony, who lived only a few miles from her in Newcastle, to take her home. Denise agreed and I set the wheels in motion.

The day of her flight to the Algarve was particularly hazardous. Much of the UK was shrouded in fog and her plane from Newcastle to London was delayed in taking off meaning she would miss her connection to Portugal. I was in the process of trying to get her re-scheduled onto a later flight when she arrived at Heathrow only to discover that the plane she had originally been booked on was still grounded. A further phone call resulted in switching back to the original booking and at last she was airborne.

There was however a further problem, when the plane's pilot ran out of flying time and was forced to land in Lisbon. Luckily there were three passengers onboard who had business in the Algarve that afternoon and, hearing that Denise also had to be there, they invited her to join them in their hire car for the remaining two hundred miles of the journey.

* * *

My life was now in turmoil. Denise had been in the Algarve for only a few days and I had no idea what might happen when she got back to England. I knew that I wanted to be with her but I couldn't see how it could possibly happen. I didn't even know if she would be able to commit her life to me, or to a part of the country that she had never been to before. We both lived so far apart but I simply couldn't imagine her not being in my life any more. I became desperate.

I awoke one morning and knew that I had to leave Lyn. She was out when I put together a few things and then did something that I have never been proud of – Lyn deserved more than that. I left her a letter before closing the front door behind me. I was clearly not thinking straight because having made such a drastic decision where would I go? There had been no preconceived plan and Denise certainly had no idea of what had just happened. I needed somewhere to stay, and with someone who might be sympathetic to the situation I now found myself in. And so on that Sunday morning I knocked on the door of John and Gloria Marshall.

I called Denise and told her the news. Her initial reaction was one of disbelief and shock followed by the regret that she was not there with me to offer support. There was still more than two weeks to go before she was due back from Portugal and I was on my own. It was a most distressing time for everyone involved. Mixed emotions played havoc with me, especially when I had to go back and face Lyn for the first time since leaving. I continued to see Christian and Natalie as it was important for them to know that I was still their dad despite what was happening between me and their mother.

The day finally arrived when Denise flew back from the Algarve. I picked her up from Heathrow and drove her to Norwich for the very first time.

The Talk was its usual busy self for the appearance of Tony Sands. Denise got herself ready in the dressing-room and then it was time for her spot. She swept onto the cabaret floor and in no time at all she had the audience in the palm of her hand;

it was good to see how they quickly warmed to her. I stood at the back of the room with everything crossed, and willing her to do well, but I needn't have bothered. Without any prompting whatsoever manager Ryan tapped me on the shoulder.

'She's the one,' he said. 'I want her as our resident singer.'

* * *

Ryan's decision meant that a future with Denise, which at one time had seemed impossible to even imagine, might now have a chance of surviving. The Talk was due to close after New Year's Eve and reopen late spring. That three month period allowed Denise sufficient time to clear her cabaret bookings up north and sell her house. It was a huge commitment for her to uproot her life and start afresh with me in Norfolk and she would certainly be stepping into the unknown.

Christmas Day was particularly hard. That night Denise was working locally in the north-east and was at home in Cramlington. I was in Norwich with very little seasonal spirit and I spent time during the day with Christian and Natalie before travelling north to see Denise. Later that afternoon, as I drove out of Norfolk and up through the fenlands of Lincolnshire, I passed brightly lit houses along the way. I imagined them to be full of happy family gatherings and at that moment I felt like the loneliest person on earth.

Denise had already left for work by the time I arrived but when she returned home later that night I was so pleased to see her. It felt as if our Christmas was only just beginning.

42

1984 was upon us and there was much to be done. The Talk had closed its doors to the public and I remained in the office trying to salvage what I could of my business. I sought legal advice and was told that I had a case against Gill for misleading people into believing that Norwich Artistes was finishing. She denied the allegation and the legal wrangling between us continued for some time. Despite all the effort and preparation the case never made it to court and achieved little other than swelling the coffers of our respective solicitors.

***

The Talk was undergoing its major facelift. The building's original interior ceiling was ripped out leaving a large gaping apex above. A new stage was built where one of the long bars used to be and the old VIP lounge was transformed into part of the new backstage area which included three new dressing-rooms and a shower. I thought that it was not just the structure that had been ripped apart; it felt as if the very heart and soul of the venue had been destroyed. The warmth and atmosphere of the place that had previously created such magic was in my opinion never again recovered.

The place itself was reputed to have been haunted and there were those who claimed to have seen the apparition of a lady dressed in grey gliding along the upstairs landing. When the club was closed to the public during the daytime I would often be the only one in the building. At the end of the afternoon I would lock my office door and switch off the upstairs lights.

I would then fumble my way in the gloomy darkness, along the landing, down the stairs and through the nightclub itself until I finally arrived in the illuminated foyer. The eerie silence was occasionally broken by the sound of the floorboards creaking and groaning underfoot and I often wondered if "The Grey Lady" was keeping me company.

Denise had given her agent in the north-east notice that she was leaving and her decision was met with scepticism.

'You'll be back,' was his parting shot.

Even her father, as conservative a man as you were ever likely to meet, had suggested that she gave living down south with me a try but kept her home just in case things did not work out. Denise however was determined that her move would succeed and by February she had sold her house and moved her furniture into storage in Norfolk.

The room at John and Gloria's was cramped but had now become home for both of us. Denise helped out in the office as I faced the task of re-establishing myself as an entertainment agent.

I had prepared the programme for the Talk from the time it was due to reopen at the end of March. Des O'Connor was followed by Alvin Stardust, Bob Monkhouse, Ted Rogers, Ken Dodd, Gary Wilmot, Vince Hill and Roger De Courcey. Our resident team's first monthly floorshow was in full rehearsal.

The Friday night, before Des O'Connor's sell-out opening, we had a dummy run-through of how the following evening was to operate. The caterers prepared dinner for the Talk's directors, along with their respective partners and a handful of specially invited guests. After the dinner we performed our floorshow for them and everything appeared to be in order until someone realised that the licence, required in order to open to the public, had not been applied for. At that point it seemed as if the grand opening night would have to be postponed but director Tim Enright made a late night phone call and somehow the licence was granted the next morning.

The Saturday 31st March opening went ahead as planned. Des O'Connor was brilliant – the crowd loved it and the local newspaper featured a full page editorial heaping praise for how well the whole thing had been received by the public and heralding the birth of a new era at the nightclub.

43

I had struck up a good working relationship with the new management of the Talk, especially Silvio Markovic, who I became friends with, as did Denise with Silvio's wife Lynne. After a while they invited us to move in with them and, although we were grateful for the hospitality that John and Gloria had shown us, we welcomed the extra space that the move offered. Our social life revolved around a small gathering of people and in my spare time I turned out for a local village football team.

**

Buxton Football Club survived thanks to the endeavours and dedication of a small group of people. The Platford family were the lifeblood of the club, with Teddy acting as the team physio and wife Daphne and daughter Glenda forever organising fund-raising events and ensuring that the kit was always laundered. "Hockey," a school grounds man ensured that our pitch was always kept in the best possible condition. Barry Wortley, the drummer with Fresh, turned out with me for Buxton on a regular basis whilst a couple of cabaret acts, when working in the area, made guest appearances and donned the tangerine shirts.

Gary Wilmot may have been regarded as a highly talented and respected television and West End performer but he was just another one of the boys on the Saturday afternoon he turned out for Buxton in a bruising cup-tie encounter.

One act who featured in the first new programme of attractions at the Talk was a relatively unknown comedian and impressionist called Bradley J Walsh. Prior to him becoming an entertainer he was an ex-professional footballer with Brentford and he soon became a favourite in Norwich. Occasionally Brad would call to tell me that he had a forthcoming Saturday available.

'Okay you're booked but we have a game that afternoon,' I'd say to Bradley. Bradley Walsh made three appearances for Buxton Football Club during that 1984/85 season.

Buxton weren't just a team who had celebrities occasionally playing for them. We found ourselves with a proper footballer on our hands the day Dragan came along.

Dragan, the cousin of Silvio Markovic, was visiting Norwich for a short time. Yugoslavian Dragan was in his twenties – he stood well over six feet tall and sported a dusky Serbian tan. He had played football to a high standard in his own country and we had no hesitation in welcoming him to our club and handing him the number nine shirt. Dragan's goal-scoring ability, not only moved us quickly up the league table, he also succeeded in swelling our match day spectator attendance. The local girls in the village began to take an interest in football and turned out en masse to see him play, greeting him with hero-worshipping cries of 'C'moon Draagon!' as another of his efforts hit the back of the opposition's net.

Word travels fast in Norfolk and it wasn't long before the bigger and better teams were after his services but I had an ace up my sleeve.

Dragan was a huge fan of the former Chelsea and England centre-forward Peter Osgood, so much so that he became his role model. And as luck would have it, I just happened to have one of Peter Osgood's England tracksuits.

***

In the late seventies I was part of the organising committee for Norwich City's captain Duncan Forbes' testimonial season.

Also on the committee that year was ex-West Ham and Tottenham footballer Martin Peters who was then playing for Norwich. Throughout the season we attended a number of fund-raising events where Martin offered up some of his England shirts for auction. These souvenirs always caused a bit of excitement, especially the night when an auctioneer, clearly with very little knowledge of football, let his enthusiasm run away with itself. In an effort to crank up the bidding for a traditional white England shirt bearing the number eleven he announced that it was the actual one worn by Martin in the 1966 World Cup Final. Every soccer enthusiast knows that, for that final, England had switched to red shirts and Peters wore sixteen, his squad number.

When Duncan Forbes' testimonial season was finally over there was still football memorabilia accumulated along the way which we had never got round to auctioning. One of those items was Peter Osgood's 1972-73 England tracksuit. The tracksuit was duly handed over to an incredulous Dragan thus ensuring that we retained his services for the remainder of his stay in Norfolk.

During that year I broke my leg. At the age of thirty-seven my days of being a hustling and bustling attacking player were behind me and I was comfortably nestled into the middle of Buxton's back four. It was not more than a minute into a game in the wilds of North Norfolk when I inexplicably went into a scything tackle. A loud crack immediately followed and then a searing pain. I lay motionless on the ground until an ambulance arrived. I was taken to hospital where it was confirmed that I had broken both the tibia and fibula in my right leg.

A routine plaster cast should have repaired the damage but it didn't work out that way as the bones refused to knit themselves together and eventually I had to have a metal rod inserted into my leg. I spent twelve days in hospital and, all these years later, I am still managing to trigger off security alarm systems at airports across the world.

The following football season I became re-associated with Buxton when, as the manager of their reserve team, we achieved success in virtually every league and cup competition that we played in. Although we were officially recognised as the reserves, the side I put together was far too good for the league we played in. The squad became such a close-knit bunch, socially as well as on the pitch, that the players had very little interest in being promoted to the first team. I ignored the philosophy that a village football team should only contain local inhabitants and recruited the best players I could find, including some who were stationed at a nearby military air base. Very soon on match days the Norfolk dialect could be heard entwined with shouts of 'Over 'ere' and 'On me 'ed son,' in a wide variety of Scouse, Geordie and West Country accents.

The next year saw a major restructuring of the local football leagues and consequently Buxton found itself elevated into a higher level of competition.

Following my achievements and success with the reserves the next season I was encouraged to take on the managerial duties for the first team but my Midas touch had clearly deserted me and was never to be repeated. It became quite apparent that I was not "The Special One" after all as we finished that season in mid-table mediocrity.

44

After such a dazzling debut, the new Talk had found it difficult to maintain its pulling power. Despite the array of talent on offer the people were not turning up in the numbers that had been hoped for and, in order to reduce the expenditure, cutbacks had to be made.

Whilst we were relatively comfortable living with Silvio and Lynne, Denise and I were aware that the situation could not be permanent. Denise had become increasingly anxious that we should have a home of our own and we eventually bought a new two-bedroom house, built in a picturesque and leafy location in Brundall, just outside Norwich. We became part of a small and friendly community and enjoyed a good relationship with all of our neighbours. I think that we were probably both as happy there as we have ever been in all our years together. Our happiness would have been complete had it not been for the financial constraints by the uncertainly at the Talk. With the work there becoming less frequent we knew that we would have to look elsewhere.

Clubs and pubs might have provided the answer but Denise had no experience of singing to pre-recorded backing tapes as she had always been used to working with live musicians. The obstacle was overcome when Fresh recorded some backing tracks for her and she was up and running.

The fears that we'd had for a while were eventually realised when the Talk announced its closure as a cabaret venue and it was eventually taken over by new tenants who changed its name to Springfields. With new management now in place, the days of Norwich Artistes being allowed to continue to operate there were clearly numbered. Neville Downing came to the rescue when he offered me the use of an office within his Magic Products complex. Fourteen years had gone by since John Fisher had first asked me to join the agency and lo and behold, there I was, back in Prince of Wales Road.

I contacted everybody I could think of to make them aware that Denise and I were available for work and very soon the bookings started to come in. There was a considerable interest in Denise, who was a new name on the southern circuit, and in no time at all our diaries looked a lot healthier. We worked in summer seasons alongside people who would later go on to establish themselves as future main attractions – Mike Doyle was the Entertainments Manager at Corton Holiday Centre and Joe Pasquale was then just part of a Warners resident team near Lowestoft. We also appeared with a young Shane Richie for Stena Lines on their Harwich to the Hook of Holland ferry crossing.

* * *

Occasionally I would walk the short distance from my office into the city centre and in doing so I passed the premises of an estate agent. In the window there was a revolving column which displayed properties for sale and one of the houses on offer captured my eye. Over the next few days, as I passed the window, that same house was always at the front of the display column and seemed to be inviting my interest. The property was detached and much bigger than what we had in Brundall and it occurred to me that there would be more than sufficient room to accommodate Norwich Artistes. Working from home was something that I had never before considered.

I showed the details to Denise and she made the necessary arrangements for us to view. After seeing the house we both agreed that we wanted to buy it and we put our own home up for sale. We very quickly found a buyer and everything appeared to be moving along perfectly but, just as we were due to fly out for two weeks of shows in Tenerife, our buyer pulled out. We didn't want to jeopardise the purchase of our new home so we decided that we would say nothing to the owner until we got back.

'Leave the keys with me,' volunteered our friend Jo from across the road. "You've got a nice house, there will be other offers.' Jo was forever the optimist.

She was right. Two days after we had left for Tenerife another buyer showed up. This time there were no hiccups and the sale in Brundall went ahead.

We moved into Holt Road on 1st May 1986 and the contents of the Norwich Artistes office followed a week later. The emptiness of the house exposed a number of faults that had previously been disguised behind fixtures and fittings. The replacement of some of the windows was a priority together with treatment for woodworm in the stairs. There was also a considerable amount of electrical work that had to be carried out before we could even think about decorating and furnishing. Although we loved the house, buying the property, and then having to put right the essentials in it, had really stretched us financially.

45

Barry Rose, the flamboyant entrepreneur of Go Continental, used to promote a three-day travel show in the spacious hall at the Norwich Sports Village Hotel. All the major holiday tour operators attended and I was asked to add live music to the event – Black Lace, of *Agadoo* fame, in particular proved extremely popular with the visitors. Each day Barry held a raffle and gave away a free holiday to the winner. On this particular day it came to the time of the draw and Barry had as usual whipped the excited public into a total frenzy.

'Who wants a free holiday in Spain?' he bellowed into the microphone.

'I do!' Hundreds of people yelled back simultaneously.

'Can't hear you!' cried Barry. 'I said who wants a free holiday in Spain?'

He plunged his hand into the raffle drum and withdrew it holding a solitary ticket aloft. He then called out the ticket number.

I stood, with my own raffle tickets in hand, watching the crowd's response. Barry then announced the winning number again and I suddenly realised it was mine.

'Over here!' I signalled as I made my way to the stage waving my ticket in the air. Barry caught sight of me and screamed at the audience.

'It's Brian Russell – he doesn't need a free holiday. We'll draw it again!' The people cheered. Barry dived once more into the drum and I stood aghast as an elderly lady was helped onto the stage to claim the prize that was rightfully mine.

A working trip abroad soon after proved to be much more exerting than a free holiday in Spain would have been.

* * *

I had put together a weekend of arena style variety shows at the Sports Village, the first taking place on a Friday night featuring Bernie Clifton with me and Denise in support. The following night we were both booked for a military Summer Ball in Gibraltar and, after we had finished with Bernie, we left immediately and drove through the night to Gatwick airport to board an early morning flight. We were met in a rain drenched Gibraltar and driven to our hotel.

'Can we get some food?' I asked. 'We haven't eaten since yesterday.'

'We'll get some later,' I was told. Denise unpacked at our hotel while I went to collect a PA system that had been loaned for us to use that night. I was then taken to the venue to set the equipment up and by now it was mid-afternoon.

'Can we please get some food?' I asked once again on the way back to the hotel.

'Yes, later,' came the response.

Denise had managed to get a few hours sleep and, after a quick shower and change of clothes, we went to the venue where the guests were already assembling for dinner. As soon as the dinner had finished it was time for us to go on and by the end of the evening we were both so tired that any thought of eating had passed and we collapsed into bed.

The following day there was a family fun-day at the barracks. A local radio station was there doing a live outside broadcast and I was asked to do an interview followed by a short spot. After the broadcast we were driven to the airport for an afternoon flight back to Gatwick.

That promise of food 'later' eventually materialised. We were allowed a quick stop for a pizza on the way to the airport and we finally arrived back home on Sunday night, thirty-six hours after we had started out on our journey.

46

Ray Aldous came to see me armed with a box full of memorabilia after a clear out at his home. Inside the box were some faded black and white autographed pictures of famous stars long gone but there was one collection in particular that he thought I might be interested in.

Since 1963 Ray had coveted the title of "The Man Who Brought the Beatles to Norwich" and there were items from that memorable evening that he thought might be worth selling. He had signed autographs and photos of the band that had been taken backstage together with the actual contract for the booking signed by Brian Epstein. The most interesting item however was a reel-to-reel tape recording of the Beatles' live performance and the quality of the re-production was excellent.

I contacted Sotheby's, London's famous auction house, and told them what I had. They were very interested and a meeting was arranged. I travelled to London with the collection and, after inspecting the items, Sotheby's agreed to include them in one of their forthcoming auctions. Photos and autographs of the Beatles were fairly commonplace but the value of the package very much centred on the tape. I was asked to swear an affidavit stating that it was the original recording and, to my knowledge, there were no other copies in existence. I could not make the same declaration about the other items which I had already photocopied.

The Beatles memorabilia went to auction and was bought up by a private collector. After all these years their value will undoubtedly have increased considerably. Ray however was happy with his return from the auction – just as he was on that night when fifteen hundred people each paid seven shillings and sixpence, thirty-eight pence in today's money, to see a group that had cost him two hundred and fifty pounds to book.

When the booking had originally been made, Brian Epstein had given Ray Aldous the opportunity of taking a further date on the Beatles later that same year for double the fee he had originally paid. Ray decided against taking up the option as he wasn't convinced that five hundred pounds was a good investment for a group whose popularity might not last that long.

47

When Denise had first moved to Norwich she knew very few people. Because of my split with Lyn there were those who openly snubbed her. However two early friendships that she did strike up were with singer Tammy Jones and a hairdresser called Michael. Michael was outrageously gay – he sometimes sat in on the judging panel of the talent shows at The Talk when his outspoken views and adverse comments to some of the contestants made him public enemy number one. He became the person the public loved to hate.

* * *

One day Michael announced that he was in love. Falling in love was something that had happened to him on more than one occasion but this time he told us it was different, this time he intended to marry. Denise and I received an invite to the wedding, as did Tammy Jones, with her partner Roy.

The wedding took place inside Michael's hairdressing salon. The place was beautifully decked out with flowers and had a raised platform, which served as an altar, at one end of the salon with chairs arranged either side of a central aisle. The four of us took our seats among the congregation and waited.

Someone standing at the back of the room caught my eye and was beckoning to me.

'Michael wants to see you upstairs,' he said.

I went upstairs to the living quarters on the way passing six quite masculine-looking "bridesmaids" some with designer stubble and all of them dressed in white. Michael was standing alone in the kitchen. He looked distressed and told me that the person who was to have given him away had let him down and would I stand in?

I was lost for words by his request but I was cornered and how could I possibly say no? I rushed downstairs to inform the other three of my predicament before duly taking my place beside Michael at the back of the salon. Suddenly from nowhere came the sound of organ music playing *Here Comes the Bride*.

Michael linked his arm through mine. 'How do I look?' he asked.

'Wonderful,' I replied. I had clearly taken leave of my senses – what am I saying, no you don't I thought, I found myself drawn into the occasion and had little choice but to go through with the formalities of giving the "bride" away. The cavalcade, consisting of me and Michael, together with the six "bridesmaids," made its way along the aisle towards the vicar. At least I assumed he was a vicar – He wore what looked to be vicars clothing although the amount of sherry he consumed at the reception afterwards left me unconvinced that this was in keeping with the actions of a true Man of the Cloth. As we walked through the channel of beaming faces there were flashbulbs and cameras clicking away frantically in our direction. I tried to shield my face discreetly.

When we finally arrived at the "altar" Michael released his grip on me and I quickly took a backward step before turning and retreating to my seat.

The ceremony itself was conducted on similar lines to a normal wedding service. Soon enough came the exchanging of wedding rings and the formalities were coming to an end.

'You may kiss the bride,' the "vicar" informed the "groom" and, as the "groom" looked towards him, Michael obligingly lifted his veil.

At the reception afterwards a generous spread had been laid on for the guests. The four of us in our party had decided beforehand that we would stay for a short while before making our excuses and leaving. I was in the process of making my way from one room to another when an outstretched arm across a doorway prevented me from doing so.

'Don't I know you?' a voice belonging to the arm asked.

'No I don't think so,' I replied assuredly.

'Yes I do,' retorted the arm's voice. 'You work on the market.' I shook my head.

'I've got it. You're a taxi driver.' The arm was now clutching at straws.

I'd had enough. 'No we've never met, now just get out of way' I demanded as I prepared to push past.

'Ah well it doesn't really matter – Do you fancy a dance?'

Like the cavalry to the rescue, Denise appeared from nowhere.

'Come on we're off,' she said leading me away from the grasp of my would-be predator.

48

My summer season saw me back at most of the usual holiday parks in Norfolk and Suffolk as well as a few others that stretched out into Essex and down into Kent. It was mostly a lonesome business but sometimes an interaction with others helped lift an occasion. Spontaneous fun between acts transferred itself across to an audience, as indeed it did at the Drinking Trough at Scratby near Great Yarmouth.

***

Barry Hawley, better known to the public by the stage name of Jefferson Lincoln, was a singer and comedian who originally came from Yorkshire. Barry was a very popular act who never knew when it was time to come off and his forty-five minute spot would invariably end up extending to an hour or more. The resident entertainments team at the Drinking Trough came up with the idea of *The Jefferson Lincoln Award,* to be presented at the end of the season to the act that had performed the longest time. Barry and I appeared at Scratby on alternate Wednesday nights and it quickly became a contest between the two of us for the title. I would arrive to be told that Jefferson Lincoln had beaten my previous best time and I would then go out and add a few extra minutes to his personal longest.

It came to my final appearance of the season and Barry was in the lead. Many of the audience were caravan and chalet owners who were practically resident throughout the summer and they had all been drawn into the spirit of the competition. The Drinking Trough had proven to be an excellent venue to work throughout the season and that last night was no exception. I did a barnstorming show and it finished with calls for more. I duly went back on and after the encore, Tom the compere announced that I had fallen just a few minutes short of winning *The Jefferson Lincoln Award*.

Determined not to be beaten I promptly went back out to face the audience once more. The rule was that you weren't allowed to stay on just for the sake of it; the people had to genuinely want you back. After another ten minutes of nonsense with the crowd I was cheered past the previous best time thus ensuring the title.

I had been on stage for almost two hours and when I did finally come off I walked into the dressing room to find Denise and the four members of the house band sitting at a table having breakfast. They had clearly gone to a great deal of trouble as they were wearing dressing gowns and on the table was tea and toast and bowls of cereal.

'Oh you've finished, is it morning already?' someone looked up at me and jokingly asked.

* * *

After the usual venues and areas that I was regularly working in it felt like a refreshing change of scenery when I was asked to appear for a summer at Manor Park in Hunstanton. I was looking forward to the playing the north Norfolk coast but my season there began in unusual and unexpected circumstances.

At Manor Park the acts performed on the dance floor with the audience seated round the edge. Sitting at the very front table was a family with a screaming baby in a pushchair. Despite their efforts to calm the child the screams persisted but I was doing my best to ignore the distraction and work through it. Eventually I couldn't contain my frustration any longer and I approached the family. As I bent forward to speak to them I happened to place my hand on the handle of the buggy and the baby instantly stopped crying. I released my grip and the crying began once more. The audience thought this great fun and I ended up doing the rest of my act pulling the pushchair, and the now sleeping infant, around the dance floor. Moments like that can be priceless when they work in your favour.

When I arrived at Manor Park for my second visit the crying baby and its family had finished their holiday and gone home but in their place came a fresh challenge.

During my act I made some silly quip about the Irish which prompted a woman to leave her seat and stagger towards me in the middle of the dance floor.

'Sing about Murphy's bricks,' she said. Through her slurred and incoherent speech there was no mistaking that she was from the Emerald Isle and she then tried to dance with me in an attempt to seemingly turn the rest of my spot into a Ceilidh.

I hadn't a clue as to what she was on about but she stood her ground and repeated her request for me to sing about Murphy's bricks. The alcohol had clearly taken a firm hold of her and she became more offensive. I attempted to hold her up and tried to pacify her but her behaviour had become unruly and her comments were now directed towards other members of the audience who had shouted at her to sit down. Eventually Manor Park's General Manager John Hopkins succeeded in getting her out of the room and next day, after refunding the cost of their holiday, he asked the family to leave. After further protest the Irish woman eventually accepted her fate but her parting comment was a classic.

'What you seem to be forgetting sir,' she exclaimed to John. 'It was your beer that made me drunk.'

'We didn't think you would want to come back after the problem with the baby and now this' apologised John's wife Margaret after.

I found John and Margaret Hopkins to be warm and sincere people and I took an instant liking to them.

'I've met a lovely couple at Manor Park,' I happened to mention to Denise.

49

It was mid-summer and Denise and I had booked our first holiday away together, to The Gambia the following January.

During the peak weeks of July and August, some of the holiday parks added late-night adult cabaret to their weekly entertainment programme. I was booked for one of those and when I arrived for my midnight spot I met up with John Sutton. John was also an entertainment agent who was based in Lowestoft and he happened to be the grandson of the legendary music hall star Randolph *(On Mother Kelly's Doorstep)* Sutton.

I joined John for a drink and, as we sat there, we noticed a woman who was propped up and drinking by herself at the other end of the bar. From her appearance it looked as if her best days were behind her but she seemed intent on trying to find herself some male company. She tried to get on friendly terms with practically every man who came within her radar, whether they were by themselves or not, and as she became more flirtatious people were doing their best to avoid her. I thought that she looked a very sad and sorry figure and, to me, it certainly didn't look much fun being well past middle age and on your own.

When I arrived home later that night I told Denise about the goings on at the bar.

'What do you say we make the Gambia holiday our honeymoon?' I said.

***

We were married on Monday 4th January 1988. My split with Lyn had divided friendships with a number of people. There were those who had shunned me and stayed loyal to Lyn whilst others, who were not there to judge, had remained on equal terms with the both of us. Denise and I had made new friends and both they and my old acquaintances came together to make our wedding day a special occasion. John Sutton had volunteered his services to be my best man and there were also a handful of other friends connected to show business that we invited to celebrate with us. We were pleased to see Sid Dennis, who came with his wife Marie. Sid of course had been there at the very beginning when Denise and I first met in Skegness. Bradley Walsh also turned up at the reception to offer his congratulations.

I was particularly glad that Christian and Natalie were able to be there with us on the day, Natalie, along with Denise's niece Lucy was a bridesmaid. Denise's side of the family was represented by her sister Kim and brother-in-law Scott who gave her away. Denise looked quite striking dressed all in white and, with her downy headpiece and muff, she looked every bit my beautiful swan.

Not long after the wedding Natalie moved away from Norfolk with her mother whilst Christian remained in Norwich to finish his education. We arranged a special leaving party for Natalie at the Talk. The occasion was attended by a large number of her school friends and at this point I must say a very big thank you to Denise, and to John and Ronnie Fisher, who all pulled together to make the day so special, and I hope a memorable one, for Natalie.

50

I received a call from a woman in the legal department of the BBC regarding a television programme she was involved with called *Rough Justice*. The programme aired between 1982 and 2007 and played a big part in securing the release of eighteen people who had been involved in thirteen miscarriages of justice.

A Norfolk man had been convicted of murder and was serving a life sentence for the crime. The woman told me that it was normal for the convicted to initially protest their innocence but after a while they accepted their fate and "got on with it." This particular person however had consistently maintained that he wasn't guilty and fresh evidence had confirmed this might be the case and prompted *Rough Justice* to investigate further.

A dead woman, who the man admitted he knew and indeed had a brief affair with, was found buried on his land. A pathologist had placed her time of death at around the same time that the man admitted he had last seen her. After he had been found guilty and sentenced a witness then came forward to say that he had seen the woman, whom he'd met before, a while after she was certified to have died. It was alleged that she had been at the Norwood Rooms where the witness had recognised her with another man. He couldn't be precise about the exact date but said he remembered that the band the Searchers had appeared that night.

I had booked the Searchers in Norfolk on a number of occasions, including at the Norwood Rooms, and I was asked if I had any record of them being there around the time that the witness had stated. I didn't have anything to confirm that the appearance had taken place but, after sifting through a catalogue of microfilmed back-dated newspaper adverts, I discovered that the Searchers had in fact been at the Norwood Rooms at a time close to when the witness had suggested.

I reported my finding back to *Rough Justice* but just when it looked as if there might be a case to answer it all proved hypothetical as the principal witness died unexpectedly from a suspected heart attack.

* * *

My next brush with the legal system was equally as dramatic.

I had been called to jury service and, after being sworn in, I sat with eleven fellow jurors to hear the case of a man who had broken into a pharmacy and stolen drugs. He was also accused of peddling the drugs outside a school. The trial lasted for the best part of four days and towards the end of the week we, the jury, were escorted into a private room where we were to consider our verdict.

Once inside the room someone considered it a good idea to re-examine the drugs cabinet that had been broken into. We had already viewed the cabinet during the trial and I failed to see what extra light this might shed on a case that had guilty written all over it. However I went along with the request on the assumption that such action might demonstrate just how thorough we had been in arriving at our unanimous verdict.

Our next task was to elect a foreman and I personally considered an elderly gentleman, dressed in a smart navy-blue blazer and grey slacks, to be the perfect candidate. However there were two ladies who had other ideas.

'We think it should be you,' they said pointing at me. 'We've seen you on stage at the Talk of the East.'

The other members of the jury had no recollection of ever having seen me on stage, or indeed anywhere else before, but they nevertheless went along with the recommendation of the two ladies – somewhere in their minds they must have considered that show business and the duties of a jury foreman went hand-in-glove. That task completed we were ushered back into the courtroom where in the public gallery, a number of relatives and friends of the person charged were assembled. Some of those gathered were leaning menacingly over the balcony noting our every move. After we had resumed our seats the accused was asked to stand and, flanked by two prison officers, remained so as the judge announced for me, the foreman of the jury, to rise.

'And do you find the accused guilty or not guilty?' he asked of me.

'Guilty.' My response was loud and clear and delivered in a true thespian manner.

A cry suddenly went up from someone in the public gallery followed by a shout of 'You bastard!' and the shaking of a fist. The verbal attack sounded threatening and was clearly aimed at me, supposedly the presumption being that I alone had been the person responsible for committing the accused to a seven year prison sentence.

After the prisoner had been taken down the judge commended us the jury upon reaching what he told us was the correct verdict. I could not help thinking however that the public gallery might have been less averse to the elderly gentleman in the smart navy-blue blazer and grey slacks. Sometimes being in show business has its price.

51

By the end of the eighties, and into the nineties, it felt as if our fortunes had finally turned around for the better. We were both as busy work wise as we had ever been – Denise followed me into Manor Park at Hunstanton for the next two seasons and established herself as a firm favourite with the customers. We became the very best of friends with John and Margaret Hopkins, a friendship that proved to be long and lasting.

Considered by some agents as a newcomer to the cabaret circuit in southern England, Denise was offered more and more work and as a result of her success was travelling further afield out of Norfolk. I was thankful when we met Phil, a gentle giant of a man, who became her roadie and minder and accompanied her on her journeys for the remainder of her time in the business.

I was just as busy, one example being a particularly gruelling Christmas season when I was booked for six weeks, forty-two consecutive nights, at the Old Orchard Restaurant in leafy Harefield in Hertfordshire. It involved a nightly round trip of over three hundred miles and I would be there every evening for my 11.00 p.m. spot – returning immediately after, the car engine still warm, back home in order to be in the office of Norwich Artistes the next morning. I had regained my grip on the agency and was now looking after a large number of both old and new clients.

***

The Oil Baron's Ball was a prestigious event. It was held annually at the Ocean Rooms in Gorleston where over five hundred guests, connected to the oil industry, turned out to celebrate the inauguration of the new oil baron. For a number of years I had booked the entertainment for the event, including the likes of Mud, Showaddywaddy, Mary Wilson's Supremes, Chic, the Drifters, the Three Degrees and George McCrae.

George McCrae was the undisputed disco king of the seventies and had enjoyed worldwide success with hits such as *It's Been So Long, You Can Have It All* and *Rock Your Baby.* George's band was based in England and he himself lived in The Netherlands. "The Oil Baron's Ball" took place on a Friday night and George had made the forty-minute flight from Amsterdam into Norwich on a weekend ticket and was not returning home until the Sunday afternoon. He had booked himself into a nearby hotel and I was with him at the Ocean Rooms, when his music had the entire audience on their feet dancing during his seventy-five minute set.

He called me at home the following morning to tell me that he had brought his backing tracks with him and if a booking came in for that night he was more than happy to work. He must have imagined a local pub phoning me to say that they had been let down at the last minute and did I have anyone half decent who could step in?

The Oil Baron's Ball was not without its challenges however.

The Drifters appeared in Jersey two days prior to their booking with me for the Ball. On the Thursday morning, as they were due to leave Jersey, I received a call saying they were at the airport but unable to take off as the island was fogbound. There seemed no immediate cause for concern as there were still over twenty-four hours for the fog to clear but when the Drifters returned to their hotel they were greeted by fire engines and the building ablaze. All of their band's gear was destroyed in the fire and, in order to get them through their booking with me on the Friday, I had to beg borrow and steal all the musical equipment I could lay my hands on.

The Three Degrees had based themselves in London for a while during a UK and European tour but when their tour had finished, and with just five days before my booking for "The Oil Baron's Ball," they decided to fly home to the United States for a short visit. They returned to England from Philadelphia on the Friday morning of my event. The girls arrived safely but their luggage didn't and when I met up with them later, at their hotel in Norwich, I found out that they had little more than the clothes they were standing in.

The public image of the Three Degrees was glitz and glamour and for a while it looked as if it might be a case of *When Will I See You Again?* Undaunted however they set off on a shopping expedition around Norwich and, after buying everything they could lay their hands on that sparkled; they managed to transform themselves back into the Three Degrees, no doubt to the delight of their fans.

52

1997 and my fiftieth birthday was less than two months away. My strenuous December workload had taken its toll and I was suffering the consequences – I felt generally drained and under the weather but put it down to nothing more than the hectic schedule that I had pushed myself through.

I had been out for the evening with Nick MacCartney and Mick Elliott and we ended up at the Talk. There had been a series of charity shows, presented under the banner of *The Golden Years*, which had previously been staged at the venue. The shows had featured local bands from the sixties and seventies and another show was planned for February. The three of us immediately decided on an Edentree reunion and we offered our services. This despite the facts that Pete Holmes now lived in Southport and Roger Cooke in Newcastle! Calls to both of them however were received with enthusiasm and an agreement was made that they would be there for the event which was confirmed as 13th February.

* * *

'I'm going to try and lose a few pounds before we go away,' Denise told me one day after she had stepped off the bathroom scales. We had a holiday booked to Kenya in January followed by another, as my fiftieth birthday treat, to San Francisco a month later. I thought that maybe I could do with losing a few pounds myself and said that I would join her.

The lethargy and listlessness I had been feeling for a while had showed no signs of improvement so I made an appointment to see my doctor who took blood samples which he sent away for analysis. I then began experiencing quite excruciating spasms of pain from my backside and I knew that something was not right as my weight began to fall drastically.

It was initially considered that I might be suffering from gallstones and I was referred to a consultant who could find nothing wrong. It was then suggested that there might be a problem with my prostate and so an appointment for a further examination was made.

The day finally arrived for our holiday and we took off for Kenya. When I had first suggested a safari holiday it hadn't appealed to Denise but she went along with it for my sake and in the end she enjoyed it immensely.

At our resort we met Trevor and Diane Gosling from Wiltshire. Trevor had worked for the BBC as a sound engineer on nature programmes with David Attenborough and he knew Kenya well. We listened to some of Trevor's experiences and on his advice we booked ourselves into a mini two-day safari.

We set out for our safari to Tsavo East National Park and along the way we came across herds of buffalo and elephants as well as giraffes and a pride of lions. We arrived at our overnight lodge and as the sun began to set we watched elephants drinking at a nearby water hole.

We had intended on joining a group for a game drive the following morning and we were woken very early by the sound of mooing outside. I opened the window and was greeted by a beautiful pink misty dawn and there, just below our balcony, stood a buffalo with a lion clinging to the end of its tail. Neither made any attempt to move and it looked like a stalemate situation until more lions began to appear and the buffalo was eventually overpowered. We were later told that the end was usually much quicker but there were some lion cubs present amongst the pride and the kill had also served as a teaching exercise for them.

Later that afternoon when we arrived back at our hotel we met up with Trevor who wanted to know how we had got on.

I showed him the video that I had taken of that morning's events. Trevor had been there and seen it all before but even he could not believe his eyes when I showed him what had taken place, and especially at such close quarters.

'I can't believe you got that lucky' he commented. 'It's almost as if the whole thing was stage managed.'

Whilst we were away on holiday Norwich Artistes had been left in the very capable charge of John Hopkins. When we arrived back home John gave me my messages which included one for an appointment to have my prostate checked over.

The pain that I had been experiencing was now becoming more frequent but, after undergoing an examination, it was confirmed that the problem wasn't with my prostate.

'I'm going to refer you to Mr Speakman,' the consultant told me.

53

For our very first get-together, in preparation for the Edentree reunion, there was just me, Nick and Mick and the three of us met at my house. Mick Elliott had not picked up a bass guitar for twenty-five years and was very rusty. We put together a running order and reacquainted ourselves with songs that we had not performed together for twenty-five years. Copies of the set list were then sent to Pete and Roger and, when they arrived in Norwich, we arranged a couple of full practice sessions together before the night. Barry Wortley, who had also been a member of Edentree, was to be our drummer with Pete Holmes providing additional percussion. Nick was to handle both the guitar and keyboard parts with Mick playing bass whilst Roger and I were to share the lead vocals.

During our rehearsals I gave a graphic description of the pain that I had been experiencing which caused great hilarity among the group. The information might have been just a bit too graphic however, prompting someone to remark that 'It must be like having a red-hot poker shoved up your arse.'

***

Edentree received a great deal of publicity that week. The local newspaper recounted the history of the band in a full page spread and we went into the Radio Norfolk studios for an interview with broadcaster Andy Archer with whom we had worked when he was the resident DJ at the Lafayette nightclub in Wolverhampton. David Clayton was also there to conduct a backstage interview with us as well as recording the voice-over for our off-stage introduction.

We were pleased to learn that George and Davey were travelling down from County Durham to be with us but there was one person more than any other that I wanted to be there on the night.

Phil Beevis said that he couldn't make our evening invitation but I managed to persuade him to come along during the afternoon while we were having our final run-through. He sat on his own at the back of the room as we went through the numbers and after we had finished he stood up and gave a nod of approval before quietly taking his leave.

We had worked on a forty-minute spot that featured a running order of the Four Tops *Same Old Song,* Lindisfarne's *Clear White Light, Sherry* by the Four Seasons, the Moody Blues *Ride My Seesaw*, a medley of one hit wonders from the seventies and four Beach Boys songs, *Darling, In My Room, Good Vibrations* and finally *Barbara Ann,* which we hopefully intended using, as an encore.

There we were, including the original five of us together again for the first time in twenty-five years and we finished our set with the audience yelling for more. It felt good to be back and I was particularly proud that Christian and Natalie could be there to share the moment. Roger and Mick felt the same as their children were also present.

Afterwards we analysed our performance, just as we had done so many times in the past. We knew there were one or two things that could have been better, and we may not have been the well-oiled machine that we once were. However I was pleased with what we had achieved and glad that the performance was captured live on video.

* * *

Soon after the Edentree reunion Denise and I flew to San Francisco. We stayed in a hotel on Fisherman's Wharf and took in some of the tourist attractions, including a boat ride to the famous Alcatraz prison. On the morning of the 26th February, Denise had secretly laid on a stretch limousine to take us to the airport. There we boarded a one hour flight to Las Vegas where we celebrated my fiftieth birthday at the MGM Grand Hotel. We stayed in the Humphrey Bogart Suite in that desert tinsel town and enjoyed our brief but memorable twenty-four hour visit, including the spectacular EFX show starring David Cassidy.

We returned to the UK a few days later and arrived back in the afternoon to discover that I had missed a scheduled morning hospital appointment with Mr Speakman. I phoned and explained the situation and was told that it was necessary for me to keep my appointment and to get there as soon as I could. I arrived at the hospital where I was placed on a bed in a foetal position. A nurse then wheeled in a rumbling trolley carrying what looked like chrome bicycle pumps. Over my shoulder I caught a glimpse of the various sizes and, knowing what they were there for; I hoped that I wouldn't be getting the big one on the end!

A close, and extremely painful, examination of my bowel was then carried out and I was thankful when it was over.

'I think I may have found your problem,' Mr Speakman informed me afterwards. He told me that my bowel had collapsed and he had banded it up again.

'You might get a little bit of a discharge of blood but other than that, nothing to worry about,' he said. He also told me that when he raised my bowel he had discovered a polyp which he removed for a biopsy.

54

A series of strange events happened at our home following my visit to Mr Speakman.

Denise and I both thought we could hear people talking at the top of our stairs. We were the only ones in the house. The voices were whispered and indecipherable. An old and familiar smell of a certain blend of tobacco filled the air. I could not place it but the aroma brought back memories of my childhood.

Our electric kettle switched itself on and the television changed channels. Denise has a most logical mind, and is certainly not prone to exaggeration, so when she told me she saw a figure cross our downstairs hallway and disappear through a wall I believed her. The final straw came late one night when I sensed the presence of a physical being stood right behind me.

We related these stories to friends. One of them suggested we go and see Anna.

* * *

I made an appointment to see Anna Grant, an eminent clairvoyant, well respected in the fields of spiritualism and the paranormal. I had never met Anna before but she immediately sat me down and told me that my grandfather was there with me.

'But you know that,' she said. 'You've smelt his pipe.'

It was indeed true that my grandfather had smoked a pipe and the distinct tobacco smell that I had experienced at home I could now place and recognised as being similar to his.

'He's here to bring you healing,' Anna informed me.

But I'm not ill I thought to myself.

* * *

I received a telephone call from Mr Speakman's private secretary on Thursday. She told me that the result of the biopsy on my polyp was back and that I had bowel cancer.

'Tomorrow is Good Friday,' she said. 'There's nothing that can be done during the Easter weekend. I have booked you into hospital on Tuesday morning.'

I was thankful that I had acted in good time and had followed through on the two mis-diagnosis made for my condition. Had I not done so, the polyp revealed during the lifting of my bowel would never have been revealed.

I underwent two admissions into hospital – the first was for laser treatment to shrink the tumour and the second for surgery, which thankfully removed it without any further complications. Anna Grant had been right after all. She had informed me at our meeting that I would need two hospital visits for my healing. It was an anxious and stressful episode in my life and one that I hope is never repeated.

Up until that time Denise and I had often talked about one day getting a dog and growing old together. After I had received the wake-up call of my cancer we decided that there was no reason for us to wait any longer and we brought our plan forward.

Buddy, a seven week old Golden Retriever, arrived into our lives.

55

The Millennium was hyped up to be the celebration of a lifetime. It never quite lived up to all the expectations and as the early noughties progressed it seemed that more nails had been knocked into the coffin of live entertainment.

It had been widely anticipated that Friday 31st December 1999 would be a momentous occasion and there were those who were out to profit. With an expectation of great demand for their services many entertainers held out for obscene amounts of money whilst some venues inflated their ticket prices for the evening to astronomical levels. As a result many people decided it too expensive and chose instead to celebrate privately at home or with family and friends. In doing so they realised that they could have just as good a time, and at a much lower cost. No need to worry either about taxis or drink driving. Consequently there were those who got out of the habit of going out on New Year's Eve altogether.

* * *

With the arrival of the new millennium, the Talk of East Anglia had turned full circle.

Not long after I had moved the office of Norwich Artistes from Oak Street the newly renamed Springfields nightclub closed. John Fisher then approached the brewery and, after a period of some twelve years, the venue was once again restored to the Fisher family name. After an initial attempt to operate to the format of the old cabaret days, John decided that the time was right for him and Ronnie to step aside allowing son Carl and daughter Kym to take over the reins of the operation.

In 2001 I helped to arrange a retirement celebration for John and Ronnie Fisher. A number of the acts who had appeared at the Talk were kind enough to send congratulatory messages which were read out to the audience. The room was then darkened and candles lit in memory of those who had played the venue in the past but were now no longer with us. The opening bars of 'A candy-coloured clown they call the Sandman,' from Roy Orbison's *In Dreams* were followed by snippets of songs and comedy that over the years had brought so much joy and happiness to so many. Once again music and laughter filled the air.

At the end of the evening John and Ronnie took to the dance floor, as they had done on so many occasions in the past, to sounds of Nat King Cole's *When I Fall In Love*.

56

Norfolk is generally regarded as being a wealthy county and it contains an abundance of private and holiday homes that have proven to be very popular with celebrities and the like. The county is also home to a number of much larger houses, the country piles as they are sometimes referred to. In such places I have known aristocracy to celebrate by literally rolling back the carpets and dancing the night away.

I have always considered that the best form of advertising is word of mouth. I consider myself very fortunate that my services over the years have been recommended from one to another by those who mix in these select circles. Some of the requests I have received from them have been quite bizarre and diverse.

***

One client, a Knight of the Realm, decided to spring a surprise on his guests during a black-tie dinner he was hosting following a pheasant shoot. An actor had been planted at the table and appeared to his fellow guests to be drinking excessively throughout the dinner. Afterwards, when the host rose to speak, the actor, who by now appeared heavily intoxicated, began to heckle him. The heckling got worse and became louder and bawdier, much to the embarrassment of the other guests who eventually saw the funny side when all was finally revealed.

A prank that I had arranged for a celebration backfired on me. The client, celebrating his birthday, had asked for something spectacular which we had planned to perfection, or so we thought.

The theme of the evening was James Bond with all the trimmings. There were Bond-Girls and Oddjob and Jaws lookalikes. There was even an appearance by "Her Majesty," the royal lookalike resplendent and complete with corgis.

A helicopter was to land outside the marquee where the event was taking place. A masked assailant was then to rush in and "kidnap" the host at gunpoint – the pièce de résistance being the whisking away of the "captured" person on a hoist suspended from the helicopter. It had all been very thoroughly researched, and highly expensive to set up, so what could possibly go wrong?

The evening was in full swing as the chopping sound of helicopter blades got louder and closer. The landing was perfect and the attacker jumped out with gun in hand. He rushed towards "The Birthday Boy" who barely had time to hold up his hands in mock surrender before a guest, full of intoxicated bravo, leapt forward and smashed a bottle over the kidnapper's head. The precision planning that had taken place beforehand had made no allowance for the possibility that there might be a hero among the guests.

Thankfully the attempted "kidnap" plot didn't end in tragedy. Everyone at the party had a great time and considered the stunt quite brilliant, including the bit with the smashed bottle that people had assumed to be part of the action. Luckily for him, "The Villain" was wearing a safety helmet and so lived to kidnap another day.

* * *

Burnham Market is a tiny Norfolk village situated twenty miles to the north-east of Kings Lynn. It has less than a thousand inhabitants but such is its popularity among the elite that it is sometimes referred to as Chelsea-on-Sea. Paul

Whittome should rightly take a great deal of the credit for Burnham Market's rise in status.

Paul was the proprietor of the Hoste Arms, the village's country pub and restaurant. His education included private schooling at Uppingham in Leicestershire where he became friends with the actor Stephen Fry. At Burnham Market Paul was a popular larger-than-life character and, thanks to him, the Hoste Arms attracted personalities from all over.

In 2007 I was asked to provide musicians to play for Stephen Fry's fiftieth birthday, the party being held at the Hoste. The musical theme for the evening was based around the 1930's and forties – in keeping with the TV series *Jeeves and Wooster* in which Stephen had starred with his friend Hugh Laurie. Prior to his birthday, Stephen Fry had been filming a series of *Kingdom* but bad weather in Norfolk had caused a delay in the production. The programme was finally completed on the actual day of his birthday, 24th August, and Stephen was then collected from the location in the market town of Swaffham and driven up to Burnham Market where he joined a bevy of celebrity friends who were there to help him celebrate his special occasion.

Paul Whittome was constantly looking for ways of lifting the profile of the Hoste and announced one day that he was to open a Business and Conference centre at the establishment. His South African wife Jeanne was an interior designer and she had themed the centre with her homeland very much in mind.

'Do you have any Zulus?' Paul asked.

Who doesn't I thought, as if Paul had considered that requests for Zulus was an everyday occurrence. In all my years in the business I had been confronted with many different and unusual challenges but recreating the battle of Rorke's Drift in a North Norfolk village had not been one of them.

I began my quest to track down Zulus and followed leads that eventually led to London where I discovered a real live Zulu. His English was poor but he did possess a mobile phone which apparently promoted his status to Chief of England's Zululand. I told him what I was looking for and his English seemed to improve when we finally got round to discussing money. "Deposit" being a word that featured in his limited vocabulary.

'Where do we have to go?' he wanted to know after the negotiations had been concluded.

'Do you know where Norwich is?' I asked him.

He thought that he might possibly have heard of Norwich but he clearly had no idea where it was so I figured that there was little chance of him finding Burnham Market.

'You get on the train at Kings Cross station in London and get off at Kings Lynn,' I told him, having arranged for a driver to collect them and take them to the Hoste Arms.

The day of the official opening of the Business Centre arrived and four Zulus boarded the train in London. Early that afternoon I received a call from the driver who had instructions to pick them up.

'Is that Mr Russell?' he said. 'I'm at Kings Lynn station and the Zulus aren't on the train.'

I had a poor mobile signal so it took several attempts before I was eventually able to make contact with the Chief Zulu who told me that they had got off the train at Cambridge by mistake. I told him to take the next train and that someone would be waiting for them in Kings Lynn. Not long after the thought occurred to me that the next train might not in fact be going to Kings Lynn – by now they could well be on their way to Timbuktu for all I knew. I called the Chief's mobile again but this time there was no signal. The next Cambridge train was due into Kings Lynn at 5.15 p.m. and all I could do now was wait and hope.

Just before five o'clock my phone rang. The Zulus were at Kings Lynn station and there was nobody there to meet them.

'Wait there, don't go anywhere,' I told them.

A number of distinguished guests had been invited to Burnham Market for the opening of the Business Centre. After

Amanda Holden's welcoming speech the sound of beating drums began and no-one was more relieved than me to see four Zulus dance their way into the courtyard. The three male members of the troupe were each wearing full battle dress, complete with their shields and assegais, whilst the fourth member, a female, was resplendent in a colourful tribal outfit.

One of the male guests sidled up to me.

'Do you think she'll go topless?' he whispered.

I have never had a single enquiry for Zulus since that day, which is just as well because soon after the Chief Zulu, along with his mobile phone, vanished into thin air. Quite how they had managed to arrive at Kings Lynn Station ahead of the train remains a mystery.

* * *

One of the most lavish events that I have ever organised in my career was for a fortieth birthday bash held at this particular gentleman's country spread. It was a magnificent event, self-indulgent in the extreme.

The guests who arrived at the party late afternoon were greeted by Beatrix Potter characters poking their heads through the hedgerows leading to the property. At the car park they were met by fire-breathing angels on stilts and a trail of purple carpet meandered its way through an avenue of semi-naked living statues and into a courtyard, where champagne and canapés were served. A palm court orchestra played in the background. After the drinks reception the guests were escorted into a marquee for dinner.

Following the dinner the marquee became bathed in pink lighting whilst Drag Queens, acting as cigarette girls, mingled amongst the tables. Specially imported giant butterflies were then released into the air and, with their flapping wings took on the images of tiny fairies as they flew high into the marquee's canopies.

The musical *Moulin Rouge* was a particular favourite of the host's and a production company, which included dwarves, was recruited to present an abridged version of the show. Before *Moulin Rouge* an aria was performed by a singer who had previously appeared at the Sydney Opera House.

At dusk the guests filed outside and were treated to a firework display. The house itself had been spectacularly lit against the night sky and was covered in projected images of fairies and other creatures of fantasy that appeared to slither along the lawns and up and over the house.

Once back inside the marquee the party got into full swing as disco music filled the dance floor. A catwalk was assembled and the guests abandoned all inhibitions, including one male who had discarded the trousers of his pin-stripe suit in favour of stockings and suspenders. He led a procession strutting their stuff to the Madonna anthem *Vogue*.

The party was considered to be of such high profile that there was even talk of a feature in *Hello* magazine. A helipad had been prepared beforehand in anticipation of the possible arrival of a VIP guest, rumoured to be Elton John. Unfortunately the VIP guest didn't show; if it was to have been Elton John there might well have been a good reason as to why he had to be somewhere else that night.

Saturday 21st June 2003, the date of our party, just happened to coincide with the twenty-first birthday of Prince William.

One particular guest that evening was impressed enough with all he had witnessed to ask if I would repeat the experience for an event he was hosting at Syon Park, the London home of The Duke of Northumberland.

57

Any organisation that provides social gatherings for its employees should have a Colin Veitch. Colin was the person responsible for overseeing the events for John Lewis and he was the most endearing of people. He had abounding enthusiasm for his job and during the Christmas season it was not uncommon to catch a sighting of him, dressed as Santa, on a motor bike up and down the highways delivering presents.

When Disney's *Mary Poppins* opened at the Prince Edward in London, Colin hired the entire theatre for the John Lewis partners. In keeping with the theme of the production he booked real chimney sweeps to escort the partners along Old Compton Street and into the theatre while golden stardust was being sprinkled upon them from above. It was a spectacular and personal triumph for Colin, but not without cost to John Lewis. The Partnership later received a bill from Westminster Council for cleaning up the mess caused by the stardust.

One summer Colin asked me to organise a day trip to Weymouth. As the partners arrived early morning at London's Waterloo station, they were greeted by music from a jazz band. On the train they were further entertained by clowns and magicians who performed along the aisles during the three-hour journey to the seaside town. On arrival in Weymouth there were more musicians waiting to perform for them. Their day in Dorset included a stroll along the promenade, a paddle in the sea, fish and chips and Punch and Judy on the beach. Everyone came home happy and a good time was had by all.

'*Strictly Come Dancing* is popular,' Colin called to tell me one day. 'I think we might give it a go.'

Warners Littlecote House Hotel in Hungerford, Berkshire was the perfect location for the weekend event and I gave thought as to how we could create our own version of the television programme. The first thing we considered was the use of the show's title *Strictly Come Dancing* and in order to avoid any conflict with the BBC, we called ours *Strictly Come Dancing Take to the Floor.* I booked a twelve piece band to provide the live music and hired instructors from a local dance company who agreed to provide daytime ballroom lessons on the Saturday and Sunday. A dance competition was to be held on Sunday, the last night, when the instructors were to act as our judges. All I needed now was to find a head judge, someone who could also host the final.

Lionel Blair had been a popular song and dance TV personality in the seventies and eighties and I considered him the perfect candidate for the role. I booked him and arranged for a driver to collect him from his Surrey home on the Sunday afternoon and take him to Hungerford.

A few days before the event I called to confirm the arrangements.

'And you are picking Lionel up from Blackpool?' his manager said. I found out that Lionel was hosting a BBC touring version of *Strictly* at the resort on Saturday, the night before my booking.

I reminded his manager that the arrangement was to collect Lionel from Surrey and I had no intention of sending a driver all the way up to Blackpool. Lionel then came up with the excuse that he would not otherwise be able to get back in time but I had already made enquiries and knew that a London train was leaving Blackpool late Sunday morning which allowed enough time for him to get home and be ready. Deal done!

The dance weekend was an outstanding success and Lionel Blair proved to be absolutely charming. He acted as compere for the evening and, as the head judge he drifted amongst the couples on the dance floor, occasionally interrupting a male contestant to take up the dance with his partner.

How the ladies loved that.

58

Throughout my younger days and into mid-life I'd always considered myself to be reasonably fit and healthy apart from a few sports injuries such as broken bones and hernias. I had experienced a few heart flutters several years before but the first warning of any reoccurrence happened while Denise and I were on holiday in the Far East. We were staying in Chiam – over two hundred kilometres by road south-west of Bangkok, when I awoke one morning with severe palpitations. I had a rapid and irregular heartbeat and eventually a doctor was called. After he had given me an electrocardiogram he prescribed some tablets.

When we arrived home I saw my own doctor who told me that the medication I had been given was for angina, which I didn't have, but it was confirmed that I did have atrial fibrillation, or AF as it is commonly known. The upper chamber of my heart was not functioning properly which put me at risk of a stroke and so I was prescribed a daily dose of blood thinning tablets.

***

The arrival of Buddy our Golden Retriever had certainly altered our lives. For the first time since Denise and I had been together work ceased to be the predominant force in our lives. Denise, me and our dog became a family and we enjoyed country walks and play time together. Buddy was simply the greatest companion to have around. During the first warmth of spring he chased rabbits up and down the hills of our local heath. In the summer he splashed and swam in the river and he danced among the avalanche of fallen leaves that I flung over him in the autumn. When winter came he loved to catch my thrown snowballs in his mouth as I rolled him a snowman. He gave us both so much pleasure and he became a personality in his own right when he was photographed and chosen for the front cover of W H Smith's Millennium puppy calendar.

Not long after Buddy's glory as a Calendar pin up, I too had my moment when I received a call from local BBC radio presenter Roy Waller. Roy invited me to be a guest for a one hour programme that he wanted to air about my life. Things were certainly looking rosy all round as the business of Norwich Artistes continued to move along the right path and grow. Managing Director John Hopkins entrusted me with booking all the entertainment into two of Oakley Leisure's prime venues that stretched down into Sussex. Whilst this occasionally resulted in long and tedious drives for meetings it gave me an opportunity of introducing some new acts for Oakley's holiday makers. Shane Richie, the Brother Lees and Bradley Walsh were just three names who were added to both parks list of forthcoming attractions.

* * *

I have always appreciated additional work that has come my way but experience had taught me not to take work for granted. The entertainment business, just like any other industry, can be unpredictable. There are fickle people who change like the weather – they switch their allegiance without a moment's hesitation or consideration of the good work and service that you may have given them in the past. They use your knowledge for their own gain and, when they think you are expendable, they move on. Equally there are those who are the opposite. They are the ones who maintain their loyalty which in turn facilitates a valued and trusting working relationship.

I am proud of the many hundreds of events that I have organised for the hotel, holiday, corporate and private sectors over the years but I gained equal satisfaction from working with individuals who strived to make their own enterprises successful.

Rodney Cheeseman was a prime example. His Wheelstop Restaurant at Scratby resembled an American drive-in diner and had a reputation for good food, but it was Rodney's charismatic personality that really turned the place into such a popular venue. The restaurant was a veritable shrine to the late Buddy Holly – his photographs and record covers were displayed throughout the building and a Wurlitzer jukebox took centre stage in the main seating area. During the Christmas season I put together a programme of DJ's and cabaret acts that Rodney served up alongside his festive menu. His customers, who attended in great numbers, certainly knew how to make merry.

Through our business association, I became great friend with Rodney and his wife Marie. From Norfolk to a time in Florida, where the four of us happened to be at the same time, Denise and I spent many a happy hour in their company. There were times spent by the four of us in the small hours of the morning as Rodney and I sang ourselves hoarse to almost every sixties song we could think of.

Trevor Wicks was another who was a pleasure to work with. He was a film buff from an early age and in the 1990's he realised a boyhood dream when he acquired the Odeon cinema in Norwich which he renamed the Hollywood. He redeveloped the spacious auditorium into four smaller cinemas with Screen One being the largest and seating almost five hundred people. The acoustics, together with the large stage area, made it an ideal venue to present live shows.

I booked different genres of shows for Trevor at the Hollywood. There were tribute acts, which mostly attracted young girls who turned out in force on a Sunday afternoon to scream at their latest make-believe teenage pop sensations. We also staged concerts and theatre-style productions that included Warren Mitchell in *The Thoughts of Chairman Alf* and *An Evening with Hinge and Bracket*, which featured George Logan and Patrick Fyffe with their brilliant portrayals of Dr Evadne Hinge and Dame Hilda Bracket respectively.

There was one name however that I booked into the Hollywood who proved to be a big disappointment.

Danny La Rue was headlining in *The Good Old Days*, a music hall variety show and late afternoon on the day of the performance Trevor called to tell me that Danny was refusing to appear. The problem was the distance between the stage and the dressing room which was located down two short flights of stairs. After a great deal of haggling we eventually reached a compromise whereby a small store room adjacent to the wings of the stage was cleared for Danny's use as an impromptu dressing room.

The Danny La Rue that I watched that night was not the same person I remembered him to be from his heyday. His performance was laboured and lacklustre and he showed little respect for his audience, or indeed for Trevor who was the one paying his wages. I had left some photographs in Danny's dressing cupboard for him to autograph but immediately the show had finished he was gone leaving the pictures unsigned.

I later discovered that the reason Danny had refused to use the lower dressing room was because his feet were badly ulcerated and he would have struggled to cope with the stairs. I had every bit of sympathy for Danny's condition and understood his predicament. In common with other acts I could name however, it appeared to me that Danny had tarnished his reputation by soldiering on with performances that were now clearly past their classy best.

Trevor Wicks also presented a vibrant programme of films. From time to time, whether it was for a film premiere or some special anniversary, I would book him a Marilyn Monroe. Marilyn was the true symbol of Hollywood and her lookalike would act the part and mix and mingle with the public.

Trevor was also responsible for organising an annual film festival at another of his cinemas in Great Yarmouth. For one of the festivals I booked the comedy actor Jack Douglas to make a guest appearance for the showing of a *Carry On* film in which he had featured. Jack asked if he could bring along a friend and the former rock star Rick Wakeman turned up. The two of them seemed a most unlikely pairing but it turned out that they had met through a mutual friend, Norman Wisdom, and the shared love of comedy had drawn them together.

Other guests appearing in future film festivals included Jess Conrad, who agreed to stand in after I had tried to secure the services of sixties singer John Leyton. John had moved to Hollywood and featured in the film *The Great Escape* which Trevor had planned on showing. Another year Toyah Wilcox proved to be an extremely popular and engaging guest when she made an appearance for the viewing of her 1979 classic feature *Quadrophenia*.

***

It was not only the agent-client relationship that made the business enjoyable. The camaraderie between the acts at some venues was certainly a key factor and that contributed to much of the success of the travelling variety shows. There was an abundance of outlets such as social clubs and village halls that put on such events. The shows would consist of four or five acts and were always well supported by the public, usually selling out and consequently keeping a lot of entertainers in regular employment. From my own point of view they served me very well over the years; I could compere an evening as well as performing my own separate spot, supplying the sound and lighting for the show in the bargain.

Phil Lowen was one visual comedy act who featured a routine based on the film *Titanic*. He made his entrance with the bow of the ship, held up with braces, around him. Phil played the part of Jack (Leonardo DiCaprio) and Rose (Kate

265

Winslett) was a blow-up doll dressed in green and wearing a diamond necklace as featured in the film. During the famous outstretched arms love scene between Jack (Leo/Phil) and Rose (Kate/blow-up doll) at the bow of *Titanic,* the routine ended with Phil whispering romantic nothings to the blow-up doll who proceeded to throw up over the side of the ship. Phil was part of the show I happened to be compering at Long Melford village hall and when he arrived that evening he had an anxious look about him.

'Will you keep an eye on Rose' he asked me. 'She's got a slow puncture.'

Before he was due on Phil had inflated the doll and there she sat, erect against a wall and in all her refinery. I knew the part of his act when *Titanic* happened and five minutes before it was due I went into the dressing room to check on Rose. She looked a sorry sight – her once firm and shapely latex body had become saggy and crinkled and I knew that immediate action had to be taken.

I was on my knees, with my head up Rose's dress searching for an appropriate place to blow into, when the dressing room door was unexpectedly opened revealing my position to a number of the audience. Thankfully they all saw the funny side but my efforts had been unsuccessful and, to the song *My Heart Will Go On,* Rose made her stage appearance looking more like Kate Winslett's granny.

* * *

My irregular heartbeat was causing me increasing anxiety. I was trying to carry on as best I could but working day and night was taking its toll and leaving me drained. Pushing the problem to the back of my mind, and trying to ignore the issue, I continued to work, appearing in theatre shows with Jim Davidson, Duncan Norvelle, the Troggs and Brotherhood of Man as well as the bread and butter clubs and now more increasingly pubs.

I found the pub bookings particularly monotonous and boredom crept in. I sometimes persevered for two hours or more of an evening, giving my all to entertain an audience that was often far from receptive. I tried to pull out all the stops by bringing something different to those venues – I was including visual comedy impressions and, on my birthday one year, I persuaded Brian Poole, of Tremeloes fame, to make a fleeting appearance and join me at the Iron Duke where he performed his hits *Candy Man*, *Do You Love Me* and *Someone Someone* to a handful of dumbfounded locals.

In general, working to the backdrop of a dartboard was not for me. I don't wish to sound disrespectful to such establishments, and I know acts who have spent a lifetime making a living from such places, but it was clear that me and public houses were not a good fit and almost forty years after I had started out with the Dark Ages, I decided that enough was enough and called time on Brian Russell the entertainer.

59

I can't ever remember growing up as a sulky child and I think that the mood swings that came later in life possibly kicked in when I was middle aged. For much of the time I was full of brightness and enterprise but when the moods took over I changed from being logical and consistent into a person who saw nothing but doom and gloom and managed to turn everything that was positive into negative – my pessimism always seemed to outweigh any optimistic thoughts that I may have had. Over the years it got progressively worse and it felt as if I was being dragged into a deep dark hole from which there was no way out. I suffered bouts of severe depression and was in a bad place mentally until eventually a feeling of total worthlessness took over.

Was this my so-called mid-life crisis? I put on a brave face and to most people I might have appeared to be the same person they had always known but those close to me could see the change. My condition gradually became worse and reached the stage where just being in a crowd disturbed me greatly – I remember a time when I hid myself in a doorway to escape a passing throng of busy city shoppers. I reached my lowest ebb when I started to contemplate suicide and I considered that the world would be a better place without me. I felt desperately troubled and that I let, not only myself down, but also Denise who, despite all that was going on around her, did everything she could to cope with my irrational thinking and behaviour. I was not her most favourite person at that time but thankfully she had Buddy whose companionship and loyalty were the only bright stars in her life.

I knew I needed help but Prozac was not the answer.

'Why don't you try Chinese medicine,' our friend Margaret suggested and so I was introduced to Patrick Buzugbe.

* * *

Patrick had previously worked in a psychiatric hospital before moving on to practise alternative medicine. After giving me some initial counselling, he recommended that I undergo a course of treatment by acupuncture.

For the next three months Patrick stuck needles in me as I lay on a bed. At the very first session of acupuncture I felt a sense of relief and as the acupuncture continued my moods lifted. The feelings I'd had of defeated, inadequate and defective, that had made my life such a misery for so long, slowly began to leave me.

I still occasionally slip back into a state of depression although I feel that I am now able to deal with it a lot better than I could before. When those moments occur I know that I am not the nicest person to be around and it puts a tremendous strain on Denise and our relationship. I do have to thank Patrick for where I am at this point of time, however unpredictable it may sometimes be. His treatment worked more than any prescribed medicines could ever have done.

* * *

As if those dark days were not bad enough my heart problem had become worse. There were times when it flipped out of rhythm so badly that I had to be taken to hospital where Flecainide would intravenously be fed into my system to bring my heartbeat back under control.

I awoke Denise in the early hours of one morning to tell her I needed to go to hospital. An overnight bag was permanently packed for such emergencies and she made the usual 999 call as we had been advised to do. Minutes later an ambulance appeared in the driveway.

'I thought I recognised the address,' I heard a female voice exclaim – 'that's where Buddy Russell lives.'

Caroline had previously worked at the veterinary practice where we had taken Buddy until she decided that the medical profession offered her more of a challenge. It certainly wasn't Buddy who needed her attention that night and I was rushed to hospital on another rescue mission with the blue lights of the ambulance flashing through the darkness.

60

Two days after his sixty-first birthday in May 2001, I received a call mid-morning from one of his neighbours.

'Have you heard the news?' he said. 'Phil has died.'

Phil Beevis was gone and I was devastated. Although we hadn't seen much of one another in later life our business and sporting interests had kept us in touch.

'Have you got the cricket on?' Phil would call and ask when a test match was being played. Although he never embraced modern technology deeming most of it to be just gadgetry, Phil was not averse to making use of my computer when he needed to make a booking. He would phone and ask me to enquire of my "toy" as to who was available for a show on such and such a date.

I was pleased to see Phil at Edentree's reunion and delighted when he and Linda accepted an invitation to one of our summer garden parties at home. That Sunday he accepted a beer upon arrival and sat quietly but, as the afternoon wore on, he gradually relaxed in the company of old friends and became more like the Phil Beevis I remembered of old.

'I'll take a scotch now Brian,' he said when offered another beer and I knew he was back.

I felt privileged when Phil's wife Linda allowed me to give the eulogy at his funeral. It was both a sad yet joyous occasion as a large gathering of old acquaintances from the music industry joined Phil's family and friends in remembering a truly wonderful person who will forever have a special place in my heart.

***

When I look back to those times I am made even more aware of my own mortality.

I had been fortunate enough to have survived my cancer scare and now there I was facing a heart condition. Nowadays I am often accused of not taking enough care of myself – Denise is always telling me that I need to hydrate and drink more water. I am nevertheless reminded of just how precious life is when I think of some of the people from my past who have not been as fortunate as me.

Steve Goodrum, our drummer with Phoenix, passed away at the age of forty-seven. Even towards the end of his life he had maintained his dry sense of humour. A friend, visiting him one day in hospital, had remarked how expensive it was to use the car park.

'Really,' said Steve when told of the cost. 'That's the most anyone has ever paid to see me.'

Allan Mills, the most articulate of comedians, gave up the business in order to live out his retirement years in sunny Spain. The night before he was due to leave England for his new life abroad he had dinner with friends. He went to bed that night and never woke up again.

Sandy Sandford, Anglia TV's Uncle Sandy and later the host of Vauxhall Holiday Park in Great Yarmouth, left in equally tranquil circumstances – falling asleep in his chair whilst watching the six o'clock news.

Sandy's wife Mary died in 2004. She had always wanted to see the musical *Les Misérables* and a friend of mine, who was appearing in the London production, arranged for tickets. I took her to the theatre and afterwards we said our goodbyes as I put her into a taxi for home. Less than six months later I said another, but this time a final, farewell to Mary at her funeral.

Roger Cooke and I had shared many memorable up and down moments together on the road with Edentree. Roger was the youngest of us five band members and yet how cruel was it on both him and his family that he should be the first of us to go.

Chubby Oates' death was quite tragic and may possibly have been avoided had a correct decision been made.

On 10 November 2006 Chubby had appeared at a showbiz luncheon alongside Roy Hudd and June Whitfield. He was returning home by tube that evening when he got off at his station and collapsed on a footbridge. A passer-by raised the alarm but instead of an ambulance a police car turned up and, assuming he was drunk, they took him to sleep it off in one of their cells.

That night Chubby died of a heart attack. Had his cell been a hospital bed his life might well have been spared.

John (Randolph) Sutton's life had largely been a whirlwind of fun and laughter spent in the company of family and friends. In complete contrast his was a sad ending as when his passing came he was found at home all alone.

Neville Downing was the man who lived for fun and was forever the joker. He loved life and became so angry at the end when he couldn't accept or understand it was to be taken from him.

John Marshall, musician and my ex-landlord, together with his wife Gloria and Trefor Thomas, the other half of John's duo Twice as Nice, all played a part in my voyage of life – and all three of them passed away within a relatively short time of one another.

Ray Aldous went from starting out as a tailor's assistant to becoming a successful self-made businessman. Despite all his various ventures and achievements, Ray will perhaps always be remembered as the person who brought the Beatles to Norwich."

Jim Bowen's funeral coincidently took place on the same day as Ken Dodd's. In contrast to the thousands of people who lined the streets of Liverpool to remember the Knotty Ash comedian, Jim's took place in the peaceful surroundings of the Lake District. It was a small and private affair and a joyous occasion as a few of us gathered to recall so many happy memories of times spent together.

I knew John Fisher for over fifty years. Seventeen years of retirement had passed by since his days of the Talk of East Anglia and John enjoyed filling his time with family get-togethers, meeting up with mates in his local pub, holidays in Tenerife and making never-ending improvements to his garden. John's end came so quickly and within weeks of him first feeling unwell.

To all of those people, and indeed to any others I have not mentioned, I say a big and sincere thank you for all the memories you have left me with as I continue with life's journey.

61

In 2006 I was asked if I could provide some entertainment for a New Years Eve party at a hotel in Dubai. The enquiry was for three tributes acts and I suggested Cher, Madonna and Elvis. And so my brief but eventful association with Christtom Thomas began.

The New Year's Eve event had been successful and Christtom was now looking to book bigger attractions. He showed little interest in the flourishing tourist trade that was developing in the hotels along the ocean shoreline and instead preferred to focus his business more on entertainment for the local Emiratis.

He asked me about booking the Rolling Stones, Elton John and even the real Madonna and he became increasingly frustrated when I tried to explain that stadium acts of that stature were contractually tied up with international pro-moters and out of his reach. The fact that he appeared to have significant financial clout made it even more difficult for him to understand what I was telling him and why he couldn't have what he wanted.

Christtom then enquired about the Tupac Tenth Anniversary World Tour. Tupac Shakur was the American rapper who had been assassinated in 1996 and the tour was to be in his memory. The package line-up consisted of rappers Mopreme Shakur, who was the brother of Tupac, Big Steele and Big Syke supported by DJ Coke-e. I mentioned to Christtom that there might be a problem in putting on such an event as Tupac himself had faced all manner of criminal charges during his short life. He had contravened practically every ruling that applied to Dubai, regarding sex, drink and drugs.

Initially it all seemed like a pointless exercise but nevertheless I made enquiries and determined that a date could be made available for a show within the United Arab Emirates. The next thing was for me to provide a written undertaking to the Dubai authorities, that I would be responsible for the behaviour of the Tupac members should they be granted a licence to appear. I was still convinced that it would all come to nothing but I had no intention of rocking Christtom's world as he continued to talk about booking multi-million dollar acts. Imagine my surprise then when a call from Christtom came through early one morning informing me that he was at the government office and had been given the go-ahead for the show to take place on Friday 27th April 2007.

I was under no illusion that the ride from then on would be easy – I knew that dealings in that part of the world could sometimes prove difficult and a contract was sometimes considered to be no more than the next stage of negotiation. I had been told the story of one unscrupulous trader who had foolishly mistaken Emirati naivety for ignorance. After taking money under false pretences for a service he was unable to provide his greed brought him back into the country for what he thought were further rich pickings. The consequence of his earlier actions however led to imprisonment on his return. By now Christtom had taken me into his trust and regarded me as a brother but I was treading lightly and taking nothing for granted.

I emailed confirmation of the Tupac booking across to Dubai and was astonished when, just hours after sending the contract to Christtom, the document came back signed together with a sizeable deposit transferred into my bank account. The deal was on.

Three days before the date of the show I flew into Dubai early one Tuesday morning. I was met at the airport by Christtom and an envelope containing a fat wad of dollars was placed in my hand.

'That's the balance owing,' said Christtom.

The plane bringing the members of the Tupac tribute show was due in from Miami early that same evening and I was driven to my hotel in Dubai's Old Town district where I managed to catch up on a few hours sleep.

Christtom returned later in the day to collect me and as we drove back to the airport he told me about the busy schedule that he had prepared prior to the event taking place. He had arranged for seven television and radio interviews, including three in Arabic, together with whistle-stop visits to two of the largest universities in the region where it was hoped to pick up some additional last minute ticket sales.

At the airport the Miami flight arrived on time. I went into Arrivals to welcome everyone and as they came through I noticed that there was one person missing.

'Where's Mopreme Shakur?' I asked.

'Mo ain't on the plane, he couldn't make it,' came the curt reply. Mumbled excuses were offered as to why he wasn't there but I wasn't listening as the repercussions swirled in my head. I escorted those who had made it out into the car park where Christtom was waiting. I told him what had happened but he said nothing as the passengers and their baggage were put into a coach. I climbed into Christtom's 4x4 and the two vehicles made their way to the hotel.

The silence was finally broken.

'Do you have the envelope Brian?'

I handed over the envelope containing the money knowing that we were now at the next stage of negotiation. Big Syke, Big Steele and DJ Coke-e had all assured me that the show would be just as good in spite of Mopreme Shakur's absence but that wasn't enough. Christtom reached for his mobile phone and called the hotel telling the receptionist that when everyone's passports were handed over at check-in they were not to be given back without his permission. The hotel already had mine and I began to wonder what life might be like in a Dubai prison.

When everyone was finally checked into the hotel Christtom went to leave. I asked him where he was going and he told me he was going home to bed and that he expected me to have Mopreme Shakur in Dubai the next day.

By now it was approaching midnight local time and I was on the phone with Big Syke beside me. I had Mopreme Shakur, who was in Miami, on the other end.

'You've got to get here as soon as you can Mo,' I pleaded, credit card at the ready to pay for another airline ticket.

'I need to get some clothes,' he offered as a lame excuse. 'I'll have to go back to LA first'

Christtom had already set me an impossible task. Five hours for Mopreme Shakur to get from Miami to Los Angeles followed by a further sixteen hour flight to Dubai was never going to happen. I knew there was no way I could have got him there the next day but I had hoped that I might persuade him to come in time for the actual gig on the Friday. Eventually I abandoned all hope and after I had put the phone down Syke told me that Mo himself had wanted to come but his wife, for whatever reason, had been against the idea.

I was angry that I had been put in such a position through no fault of my own and the following morning I sat down with Christtom and explained the situation we were in. He actually listened to what I had to say and eventually we both agreed that we had little choice but to go ahead with everything as planned and hope that nobody would notice there was one person missing.

And that is exactly what happened. Despite the fact that Mo's face and name appeared on the publicity nobody picked it up, or indeed mentioned it if they had. Norman (Big Steele), Tyruss (Big Syke) and Koki (DJ Coke-e) displayed exemplary behaviour during each and every one of the interviews they attended. The forbidden topics of Tupac's alleged rape, drugs and murder allegations against him, that we had done our utmost to avoid, were all brought to the fore by the interviewers but the questions were countered with answers that spoke of positivity regarding the future rather than negativity concerning the past. It all went very well, including the visits to the two universities where I realised that I had underestimated the power of rap music in that part of the world. Steele, Syke and Coke-e were treated like rock stars and were followed by a convoy of students on scooters with horns blaring wherever we went.

The event itself was to take place within the grounds of Dubai Country Club. On Wednesday evening I went to the location to discover that the staging was in the process of being erected and flight cases containing sound and lighting equipment were piled up all around. The compressed sand of the desert underfoot was almost rock hard and pickaxes had to be used to channel a long and deep furrowed line from the stage to the sound desk to house the multi-core cable. Twenty-four hours later a gantry had been built and all the lighting rigged. By Friday afternoon, when we arrived for the sound-checks, a powerful PA system was in place. In front of the staging there were secure and enclosed areas to accommodate a standing audience of over seven thousand people. It was most impressive and had all been completed so quickly.

The show itself received a tremendous reception and at the end many of the audience, which ranged from students, uniformed police and security guards to Emiratis dressed in long flowing robes wearing back to front baseball caps, gathered to have photographs taken with the three stars of the night.

When we finally arrived back at the hotel the foyer was brimming with onlookers. There were a number of women who wanted to take Steele, Syke and Coke-e off to a nightclub in the city but an anxious Christtom was having none of it.

'I don't want them out on the streets. Make sure they stay in the hotel,' he told me as he thrust a handful of dollars into my top pocket and left for home with the members of his family who had turned out for the show. With a great deal of persuasion I managed to coax both the rappers and DJ into the hotel bar but after a few drinks the lure of the nightlife outside won them over.

The next morning everyone had assembled for a pre-arranged meeting. After the euphoria of the night before, Christtom was keen for the same line-up to appear in Bahrain and Qatar as well as dates in his homeland of India. He suggested that I should act as tour manager and visit the various places beforehand in order to ensure that the accommodation and all other necessary arrangements were in place before the event.

It was a wonderful place to be, in that company on that Saturday morning and even more so after our passports had been handed back to us. Later that afternoon we were all taken for dinner to a shisha bar where the locals sat around eating and smoking from the hookah pipes.

I was booked on an early flight out of Dubai the next morning and decided that I would have a couple of drinks before bed. I was sitting at the hotel bar when I received a message asking me to vacate my room as it was needed for a large conference party who were checking in later that same night.

I protested that the room had been paid for until the next day but this counted for nothing and, after offering profound apologies, and assurances that Christtom would be refunded, I was given barely an hour to pack. When I had done so, I returned to the bar until 3.00 a.m. closing time and then took a taxi to the airport where I spent the remainder of the night waiting for my check-in.

When I got back to England none of Christtom's enthusiasm had waned. Dubai seemed to be the main daily topic of conversation with constant emails and phone calls from him. There were a number of negotiations taking place and potential bookings were in the pipeline. I had laboriously sifted through the many pages of technical riders for Kenny G, the Backstreet Boys, Kenny Rogers and Usher whilst David Cassidy's representatives from California had called to inform me that their client would be very interested in playing the United Arab Emirates.

Things appeared to be moving along very fast until; after I had received confirmation of Lionel Richie's fee, the brakes were well and truly slammed on.

The recession had hit Dubai and there were people already feeling the impact.

One of the strict laws of Dubai is that all debt owed on bank accounts, credit cards or a loan has to be cleared before people can leave the country. If not there is the risk of detention or arrest on return to the country. There was some initial panic when recession hit and stories of those who had abandoned their high-flying lifestyle. They simply packed a bag, locked the doors of their apartments and drove to the airport where they left their cars with keys in the ignition and bought a one-way ticket out of Dubai.

Christtom's backers pulled out and that was that. Although we did try to resurrect some business together regarding local festivals and cultural shows we never reached the heady heights that had once been anticipated and eventually our association drifted apart.

62

During 2007, and in between the Dubai episode and my jaunt in the desert, I was still making regular hospital visits to see my cardiologist. My condition had deteriorated, so much so that at one stage, when I needed to be monitored, it was considered too much of a risk for me to even be put on a treadmill.

Things then took a turn for the better when my heart rhythm changed from fibrillation to flutter and I was told that I could now undergo surgery for an ablation. This was a procedure that created scar tissue within the right upper chamber of the heart in order to block the electrical signals that cause a fluttering heartbeat and it was to be carried out at Papworth hospital in Cambridgeshire.

The ablation had to be carried out while I was awake and a long thin flexible catheter was inserted into a vein in my groin and guided up into my heart using x-ray. At some point during the procedure I felt intense heat in my chest and I passed out remembering nothing until waking up some time later in my hospital bed. I was later told that the heat I had experienced was due to the catheter piercing my heart which subsequently caused it to stop beating. I had immediately gone into shock and a defibrillator had to be used to resuscitate me.

At first the ablation had been considered a success but several years later it was discovered that the surgery had subsequently proved ineffective. Just when this had taken place could not be determined. What had been determined however was that my condition was now easier to manage and, with the aid of daily medication I could enjoy a relatively much better and healthier lifestyle.

* * *

In 2009 we had to sadly say goodbye to Buddy. He had given us both so much joy and happiness through the twelve memorable years that we had him and he had enjoyed a free and relatively healthy life. In the end he just got old. It was heartbreaking when his passing finally came and it took some time for us to come to terms with. He left an emptiness that I don't believe has ever been filled.

63

Now the years are rolling by me, they are rocking evenly...
I am older than I once was, and younger than I'll be that's not
unusual...
No it isn't strange, after changes upon changes we are more or
less the same...
After changes we are more or less the same

The Boxer by Simon and Garfunkel remains one of my
favourite all-time songs. On the recording the third verse was
replaced by a trumpet and steel guitar bridge to fit within the
confines of the single recording, although the verse has often
been included when the song has been performed live. I find
the words so powerful in their simplicity.

For me the last seventy-two years have certainly been rocking and rolling by, now at a pace that seems to be gathering
much more momentum.

I have certainly been through a great deal of change in my
lifetime but I do feel that underneath it all, I am basically still
the same person I have always been. I have never allowed my
age to dictate what I should or should not be doing. Nowadays
I involve myself with Walking Football which I play at least
twice a week. The people that I play with are of mixed ages
and a wiry bunch – from the kids in their fifties to us, the over
seventies and golden oldies. We all consider ourselves to be
reasonably fit and in the course of the year we go away and
compete in tournaments throughout the country. I feel
younger, both mentally and physically, than my years but I
do think I have become more cautious and wise with age.

My circle of close friends is now much smaller than it used to be but it is much more select. I do not suffer fools gladly and prefer to keep my distance from those I do not trust or have little interest in.

There remain some old friends who I find hard to let go. They are a handful of people, some I have known for sixty years or more. I remain in touch with them.

There is still the occasional get together, when Barry Wilkinson, Mike Plunkett, Michael Barnes and I enjoy a few hours of each other's company at a local ale-house. Football, the once main topic of conversation, pretty much still is. Now though discussions centring on our medications replace those we used to have about women. Barry is still active and continues to play the drums, ironically in a band that includes Nick MacCartney.

Two members of the old gang have not been quite so easy to keep up with.

Peter Batch moved to Australia some years ago. Peter has been back to the UK on a few occasions since, not least in 2019 when some of us got together for the reunion.

John Wilkes is another who has spent the past fifteen years or more away. John had, until recently, lived in America since 2003. A few years ago Denise and I visited him at his home in Tennessee. We spent a fortnight with him, first travelling up to Memphis taking in the tourist sites of Graceland, Beale Street and Sun Records before the weather took a turn for the worse and we decided instead to follow the sun. We ended up south in Alabama, en-route to Atlanta and our flight home.

In September 2015 Barry Wilkinson and I joined up with John for a two-week US road trip. We met him in Albuquerque and from there we travelled through Lake Havasu, the home of the London Bridge, Palm Springs, Santa Monica, Los Angeles, Death Valley, Las Vegas, Hoover Dam, Grand Canyon and Monument Valley before ending back to Albuquerque. Our two thousand, seven hundred miles journey took us through the six states of New Mexico, Arizona, California, Nevada, Utah and Georgia.

Soon after John moved from Tennessee, preferring instead the warmth of Phoenix in Arizona where he remained until quite recently when he made the decision to return to his roots and spend the remainder of his life in the UK.

* * *

Over the last ten years Norwich Artistes has taken a different direction. There have been times when I have considered that enough is enough and I might sell but I have decided to keep hold of the business. There might well be someone out there with new ideas, a fresh approach and the ability to move it forward, but I have been reluctant to let go. I have seen similar businesses to mine sold and fold soon after due to mismanagement.

Having been associated with Norwich Artistes for such a long time I am the name behind the business and unless something unforeseeable happens then that will probably remain the case until the end. I consider myself fortunate insomuch that nowadays I don't have to go chasing my tail for work and the client base I have is manageable allowing me time to indulge in my leisure pursuits.

After I had finished as a stage performer people would often ask me if I missed it and the simple answer to that question was no. I am convinced that it was a lot more fun in my day compared to what many of the acts nowadays experience. I'm not talking about the stars who fill out theatres and arenas but the people who, like me, were the bread and butter acts and programme fillers. The business then seemed to be more morally uplifting and satisfying and it was not always about the money. I can remember Bob Monkhouse turning down a lucrative offer to open a new shop, preferring instead to spend his day in the company of handicapped children.

Audiences in my heyday seemed to have more energy and enthusiasm about themselves, which in turn was picked up by the performer. An audience's concentration level was so much greater and an act going on last in a three hour cabaret show would be guaranteed the same respect and attention as the one that had opened the show. People wanted live entertainment and seemed much more educated in their appreciation of it. There were many communities who organised their own events, filling their venues with audiences who were always ready and willing for a good night out. A live show, with a buffet in the interval, was as good as it could get as far as they were concerned. All round there was a greater feeling of achievement and satisfaction.

* * *

Edentree's single *You Are All I Need/Call My Name* has continued to rear its face on the music scene from time to time.

In 2014 both tracks were included on the *Portobello Explosion Volume 2* album which featured various bands that were deemed to have represented the sixties and seventies "Mod Pop Sound of Swinging London." The album itself received a number of reviews and it was pleasing that one particular New York critic acclaimed *Call My Name* as 'the gem' of the album.

The single itself gained some monetary value when it became a bit of a collector's item – EBay's description: "EDENTREE – 45 Spain PS – PROMO * mint * Call My Name."

Despite originally having been released as the B side to *You Are All I Need*, the Van Morrison penned *Call My Name* has over the years proven to be the more popular number of the two – In 2017 Denise and I were on holiday in Portugal when we heard it played.

* * *

There are things in my life that I regret.

I wish that I could have been around more when Christian and Natalie were growing up. Those times only come along once and you can never get them back. Both of them have experienced set-backs in life but they have stood up to the challenges and given me three beautiful granddaughters. Christian's daughter Hollie and Natalie's Chloe and Phoebe, will I hope grow up and make us all very proud of them.

I do wish that I had gotten to know them all a lot better but the distance between us and the various circumstances are the reasons and not excuses why this has proven difficult over the years.

Denise has been steadfastly by my side for the last thirty-six years and the most supportive wife that I could ever have wished for. She often accuses me of being selfish and inconsiderate and she is probably right. It is easy to become lazy and take things for granted and I wish that I had showed her more of the care and attention she deserved. Despite our highs and lows I do feel that together we've had the best years of our lives and she is certainly the one who has kept me strong.

All in all I know that I cannot live with regrets and I have learnt to accept the hand that life has dealt me. I try and deal with what is happening in the present rather than dwell on what might have been.

* * *

It was quite amazing that the wonderful friendship Denise and I enjoyed with John and Margaret Hopkins ever got off the ground at all. At the beginning it seemed as if the only thing that John and I had in common was that we were both born on the same day, 26th February albeit five years apart. Our four backgrounds were completely different – both the upbringings of John and Margaret were gentle and nurtured whilst Denise's and mine were quite tempestuous by comparison. Yet despite all of that somehow the friendship blossomed and the four of us remained close for over thirty years. We laughed and cried together and shared confidences in the way that only true and trusted friends are able to do. Much of our leisure time was spent in one another's company and when John's health began to fail him I am thankful that we were able to help him realise his wishes to visit New York and Poland.

We certainly made the most of those two short breaks away.

In New York the four of us made it to the top of the Empire State Building and we also visited Ground Zero, where the Twin Towers had once stood. We had photographs taken together in Central Park the morning after seeing *The Lion King* on Broadway. On a rainy Sunday Denise and I boarded a Greyhound bus from Times Square and spent the day in New Jersey while John and Margaret explored the superstore Bloomingdales.

It was a chilly March when we all went to Poland. We stayed in Krakow and visited Schindler's Factory before subjecting ourselves to the horrors of the Gestapo Headquarters at 2 Pomorska Street as well as a daunting visit to Auschwitz concentration camp. Our mood was later lightened by a fifty-five levels below ground excursion to the magnificent Wieliczka Salt Mine.

One day whilst on a walkabout Denise and I discovered the beautiful St Mary's Basilica opposite the Cloth Hall in Krakow Market Square. We sat ourselves down on a long wooden pew and marvelled at all around us when we realised that we had been joined by a man carrying a brief case.

I couldn't understand why he had decided to sit so close to us when there was plenty of space to choose from until an opening in the wooden panelling near his head suddenly appeared and we found out that we were in a line for the confession booth!

***

John's health deteriorated quite rapidly towards the end of 2018 and when Denise and I left for a three-week holiday in February 2019 we were unsure what condition we might find him in when we came back. What we found was a truly resilient man who had seemingly clung on to life whilst awaiting our return. Sadly John died just two days later.

And there I shall leave it.

This autobiographical account of my life has proven to be a five year labour of love. The idea originally started with me scribbling down a few notes of my memories and along the way I have surprised myself with exactly just how much I have been able to remember. I am grateful to those who, when called upon, were able to fill in a few of the blanks but mostly the recollections have been my own. There have been times when I have pursued the writing with vigour and other occasions when I have put it to one side for months on end. At least now I can finally stop saying to people, 'I'm writing a book you know.'

I can't imagine that there will be a sequel; I am of the age when my life nowadays is far too mundane for that. If however something exciting or unexpected should happen to me in the future then you can be sure that I shall make a note of it – just in case I should forget.

New Faces audition at the Talk: Producer Albert Stevenson seated and behind (l-r) John Fisher, Jean Holdsworth (PA), me, Colin Keys (pianist), Chic Applin and David Clayton.

The agreement of the partnership with Chic Applin's agency that never happened: (l-r) me, Jill Applin and David Clayton.

Up For the Cup team representing Norwich City FC: (l-r) Graham P Jolley, Lew Lewis, Paul Trevillion, Sadie Nine, Tony, Chris and Spike (Fresh Aire).

Dressed for the part in a BBC production of *Soldiers*.

Enjoying a birthday celebration with Denise.

One of the last pictures taken of Billy Fury just weeks before his death.

Shane Richie and me somewhere at sea aboard a cross-channel ferry.

Me and Denise on our wedding day 4th January 1988.

Buddy making the front cover of W H Smith's Millennium Puppy Calendar

Edentree's 25 year reunion in 2007:

Setting a concert rig in the Dubai desert.

The stars of the desert show – rappers Big Steele,
Big Syke with DJ Coke-e.

Me with John and Margaret Hopkins on their
Golden Wedding anniversary.